OCR

Revise Sociology

OCR and Heinemann are working together to provide better support for you

Annemarie O'Dwyer
Anna Lise White

Official Publisher Partnership

Heinemann is an imprint of Pearson Education Limited, a company incorporated in England and Wales, having its registered office at Edinburgh Gate, Harlow, Essex, CM20 2JE. Registered company number: 872828

www.heinemann.co.uk
Heinemann is a registered trademark of Pearson Education Limited

First published 2009

13 12 11 10 09
10 9 8 7 6 5 4 3 2 1

British Library Cataloguing in Publication Data
A catalogue record for this book is available from the British Library

ISBN 978 0 435467 41 8

Edited by Caroline Compton-McPherson
Designed by Wooden Ark
Typeset by Phoenix Photosetting, Chatham, Kent
Cover design by Pearson Education
Cover photo/illustration © istock photo/Les Cunliffe
Printed in UK (Ashford Colour press)

Acknowledgments
The authors and publisher would like to thank Phillip Allan Updates for permission to reproduce copyrighted materials, p. 51 and p. 54.

For the O'Dwyer and Gillis family, thanks for your love and support, and to all the sociology stars out there. –
Annemarie O'Dwyer

Thank you to my family, particularly my mum, for always giving advice and encouragement and to Davino for being there. –
Anna White

Contents

Introduction

Well, congratulations for getting to this point! This is where all that hard work for the past year starts to pay off. This revision workbook has been produced to facilitate and support you in the run up to your AS exams. Remember, the main purpose of this revision workbook is to recap and revise existing knowledge. It will not replace the notes and knowledge that should have been gained from your attendance at taught sessions at your school or college and the supported reading and note taking that you should have completed from using the core text book: *OCR, Sociology AS, Heinemann, 2008.*

How to use this revision guide:

The revision workbook has been produced in conjunction with the core textbook; it is to be used to support and to test your sociological knowledge. The workbook includes all areas of the AS syllabus; Unit 1 (G671): Exploring Socialisation, Culture and Identity and Unit 2 (G672): Topics in Socialisation, Culture and Identity. The guide is split between the two units, within each unit there will be a breakdown of the topics. After each unit there will be exam techniques, example questions and exemplar answers; these will be in the Exam Café formula which you should be familiar with from the core text book.

The two units have been broken down into topics, for example the first unit (G671) includes recap and revision activities for each identity: Gender, Social class, Ethnicity, Age and Research methods. The second unit (G672) includes recap and revision activities for: Family, Health, Religion and Youth. In both units the breakdown includes a Revision checklist, Key concepts, Mix and match and a Quick fire quiz. For the second unit there is also a Theory identifier and an Apply research studies task. Once you have worked your way through the tasks you can check your answers as indicated either through the answers appearing upside down at the bottom of the page or by referring to the back of the workbook.

> *Important note!!! Try to resist the temptation to look at the answers before you have completed the activities; remember the only person you will be cheating is yourself. If you use the workbook as it has been intended then you will be able to organise and plan your revision with confidence to ensure that you get the best results.*

How to revise

Recap, Revise, Rewind

Look out for these instructive signposts throughout the revision guide:

Recap: now is the time to recap those important concepts.

Revise: it is important to revise the relevant concepts and studies and theories. Remember your answer can only be considered sociological if you include sociology!

Rewind: check the question again to make sure that you are on track and addressing the question asked.

Exam Café: After each unit there is an Exam Café section; the intention of this section is to get you focused on the actual exam. In Unit 1 (G671) all parts of the exam question are covered (parts a, b, c and d), this is repeated for each 'identity'. For each part there is a 'Good example', an 'Example to improve' and finally a 'Now try your own'. In Unit 2 (G672) both parts of the question (a) and (b) include a 'Good example', an 'Example to improve' and finally a 'Now try your own' for each topic. For both units the exam questions can be answered by reference to the material in this revision workbook and the core textbook. Furthermore, if you carry out your own reading/research or make use of the work you have completed in your taught sessions this is likely to improve the quality of your answers.

Exam skills explanation

Both Unit 1 and Unit 2 will require you to use the skills of Knowledge and Understanding (AO1), Interpretation and Application (AO2a) and Evaluation and Analysis (AO2b). Each 'part' of each unit's exam questions will require a different amount of each skill; please take note of how much each part of the question requires each skill (refer to the Exam Café section in this workbook for each unit to help you with this).

Assessment objective (AO)

- Knowledge and Understanding (AO1): the studies, theories, concepts and contemporary examples you have learned throughout your course.

- Interpretation and Application (AO2a): how well you interpret the knowledge and apply it to a given question/point.
- Analysis and Evaluation (AO2b): judgements, criticisms, appraisals and assessment of sociological knowledge.
- One useful technique to practise is that of KIE (Knowledge, Interpretation, Evaluation):
    - Do I know this? (K)
    - Can I interpret this? (I)
    - Can I evaluate this? (E)

And finally ...

After all your hard work revising and practising exam questions it is important that once you get into the exam you try to relax and try not to panic. Take a deep breath and carefully read all the necessary instructions and the exam question before you begin. Remember this is the moment that you have been working for all year, so go out there and shine like the sociology star you are!!

Revision ... Where do I start? What do I do?

There are many different ways of revising and it is important to try out different ways and find out which is the most effective for you. The following stages will help you structure your revision.

Stage one of successful revision:

- Using the revision checklists provided in this book ensure that you have a complete set of notes for each part of the course. If you find that you are missing any parts then try to obtain these either from your teacher, peers, intranet or make your own notes from the core text book.
- Go through notes and summarise them into shorter paragraphs or bullet points. Make sure that they cover the points suggested in the revision checklist and include the relevant sociologists, concepts, examples and, if relevant, theories.

Stage two of successful revision:

- Begin your revision by putting your knowledge to the test by completing the revision activities in this book. This will help you to identify any areas of weakness.
- Once you have identified the areas you are less confident with, you could try the following revision techniques to help you remember the information: flash cards (postcard size cards with key concepts, sociologists and theories on them), drawing pictures, charts and diagrams, using post-it notes around your bedroom with key sociological evidence on them. Also you could try putting notes and reminders on your mobile phone or make a recording of things you need to remember; you can listen to this on your way to school or college or when you are going to sleep. Try making informative posters; this can be particularly useful for remembering theory. Another option could be to colour code each sub-topic as this can act as a mental and visual stimulus.

Stage three of successful revision:

- Start to familiarise yourself with the layout of the exam paper; pay particular attention to the instructive words, for example if you are asked to identify 'ways' make sure you know what you are being asked to do (refer to 'Exam question key words' in this book to help you with instructive words).
- Refer to the Exam Café section in this book and have a go at completing the 'Example to improve' questions and the 'Now try your own' questions. You can use the 'Good example' as a guide to help you plan and write your answers.

Unit code and Unit title.

Time: ensure that you note how long the exam is and keep this in mind when you are writing your answers. This will help you to keep on track and not run out of time.

OCR
RECOGNISING ACHIEVEMENT

Advanced Subsidiary GCE

G671QP

SOCIOLOGY

Unit G671: Exploring socialisation, culture and identity

Specimen Paper

Time: 1 hour 30 mins

Additional Materials:
Specimen Stimulus Material Book G671 (3 printed pages)
Answer Booklet (…pages)

INSTRUCTIONS TO CANDIDATES

- Answer all of the questions.

INFORMATION FOR CANDIDATES

- The number of marks for each question is given in brackets [ ] at the end of each question or part of question.
- The total number of marks for this paper is 100

ADVICE TO CANDIDATES

- Read each question carefully and make sure you know what you have to do before starting your answer.

Read the instructions to candidates carefully. Before you begin ensure that you know what is being asked of you. Pay particular attention to how many questions you are required to answer.

You must answer all the questions.

2

Answer **all** questions.

1 Define the concept of culture. Illustrate your answer with examples. **[8]**

2 Outline and explain how any two agents of socialisation influence masculinities. **[16]**

3 Explain and briefly evaluate why young British Asians may adopt hybrid identities. **[24]**

4 Using the pre-release material and your wider sociological knowledge explain and evaluate the use of unstructured interviews and participant observation to research the experiences of young British Asian footballers. **[52]**

Paper Total [100]

Pay attention to the instructive words (define, illustrate, explain and evaluate).

In Question 4 you must refer to the pre-release material provided.

Unit code and Unit title.

Time: ensure that you note how long the exam is and keep this in mind when you are writing your answers. This will help you to keep on track and not run out of time.

OCR
RECOGNISING ACHIEVEMENT

Advanced Subsidiary GCE

G672QP

SOCIOLOGY

Unit G672: Topics in socialisation, culture and identity

Specimen Paper

Time: 1 hour 30 mins

Additional Materials: Answer Booklet (…pages)

INSTRUCTIONS TO CANDIDATES

- Answer any two of the eight essay questions.
- You may choose 2 questions from the same option or 1 question from each of two different options
- Each question has two parts.

INFORMATION FOR CANDIDATES

- The number of marks for each question is given in brackets [ ] at the end of each question or part of question.
- The total number of marks for each question is 50.
- The total number of marks for this paper is 100.

ADVICE TO CANDIDATES

- Read each question carefully and make sure you know what you have to do before starting your answer.

Read the instructions to candidates carefully. Before you begin ensure that you know what is being asked of you. Pay particular attention to how many questions you are required to answer

Only answer two questions from the options you have been taught. Do not be tempted to answer an option you have not been taught, as you simply will not have the sociological knowledge to support your answers.

You may choose 2 questions from the same option or 1 question from each of two different options.

Each question has two parts.

Option 1

Sociology of the family

1 (a) Identify and explain two reasons for the growth in single person households in the contemporary UK. **[17]**

(b) Outline and evaluate the view that the nuclear family is the ideal family form. **[33]**

2 (a) Identify and explain two types of family diversity in the contemporary UK. **[17]**

(b) Outline and evaluate the view that relationships between men and women in the family are still patriarchal. **[33]**

Note that in part (a) you have been asked to explain 'two' reasons; you will not gain marks for answering more than has been instructed.

Exploring socialisation, culture and identity

Revision checklist

You are at stage one of the revision process; the list below outlines all the topics and sub topics which you need to cover in your revision. Take the time now to make sure you have everything you need to revise this part of the course. The points referred to below can all be found in the core text book. Tick off the areas once you have revised them and track your progress through the topics.

The formation of culture

Key concepts (definitions and examples)

- Norms ☐
- Values ☐
- Status ☐
- Culture ☐
- Roles ☐

Types of cultures

- High culture ☐
- Popular culture ☐
- Subculture ☐
- Cultural diversity ☐
- Multiculturalism ☐
- Consumer culture ☐
- Global culture ☐

The process of socialisation

Key concepts (definitions and examples)

- Nature ☐
- Nurture ☐
- Primary socialisation ☐
- Secondary socialisation ☐
- Formal social control ☐
- Informal social control ☐

Agents of socialisation (understanding each one and how the above concepts apply to them)

- Family ☐
- Education ☐
- Media ☐
- Religion ☐
- Peer group ☐
- Work place ☐

The role of socialisation in the creation of identities

Gender identities

Research studies into…

- Masculine and feminine identities ☐

The creation of gender identities through…

- Family ☐
- Mass media ☐
- Peer group ☐
- Education ☐
- Religion ☐
- The workplace ☐

Social class identities

Research studies into…

- Upper class identities ☐
- Middle class identities ☐
- Working class identities ☐

The creation of class identities through…

- Family ☐
- Education ☐
- Media ☐
- Religion ☐

- Peer group ☐
- The workplace ☐

Ethnic identities

Research studies into…

- Hybrid identities ☐

The creation of ethnic identities through…

- Family ☐
- Education ☐
- Religion ☐
- Peer groups ☐
- Mass media ☐
- The workplace ☐

Age identities

Research studies into…

- Youth ☐
- Middle age ☐
- Old age ☐

The creation of age identities through…

- Family ☐
- Education ☐
- Religion ☐
- Peer groups ☐
- Mass media ☐
- The workplace ☐

Exam question key words

The following key words will be useful for you to consider once you have reached stage three of your revision. The exams for units one and two will include questions which will require you to answer in a particular way. The questions may use a number of instructive words such as 'way', 'explain' and 'illustrate'. It is very important that you know what these words mean; this will ensure that you address what is being asked of you. Take your time to read through the list of words below and then refer to the Exam Café section of this revision guide. Look at how the questions are worded and see if you can recognise which are the instructive words. Also included in the list of words below are key words that you may wish to use in your answers, such as 'patterns', 'trends', 'features' etc.

Characteristics: identify a distinctive point; for example a characteristic of the 'new working class' would be their 'individualistic' attitude.

Features: a noticeable part of something; for example a feature of the 'metrosexual' male is that they openly invest in their appearance, through the consumption of grooming products such as facial scrubs and moisturisers.

Ways: using evidence to show a choice of possible or alternative courses; for example if you were looking at two ways an individual is socialised into their gender identity, you could look at the first way through the family and the second way through an alternative agent of socialisation such as education.

Reasons: these can be opinions, judgements or underlying explanations or causes; for example traditional Marxists argue that the reason for the existence of inequality in our society is because we live in a capitalist society.

Patterns: are a set of occurrences (something that takes place) or set of features; for example according to Van Dijk (1991) there is a pattern to how the media represents ethnic minorities in a negative way.

Trends: refer to when something is heading in a general direction or where there is a general tendency to something; for example in the contemporary UK there is a trend for women to opt out of becoming 'homemakers' and to concentrate on their careers. Trends occur over time.

Explanations: this is when you use a statement or theory or fact in order to make something clear and understandable and to make an account of something; for example you could argue that the official retirement age of 65 years explains why many people see this as the social marker for the beginning of old age.

Theories: a series of ideas, principles and beliefs which seek to explain the way the social world is from one particular view; for example feminist theory believes that there will always be inequality for women in society as society is patriarchal (dominated by males).

Illustrate: this is when you make a statement clear by providing examples; for example if you are asked to define 'hybrid identities' you would define the concept then give an example such as 'Brasian' to illustrate your response.

Advantages: to emphasise the good qualities or positives of something; for example one advantage of 'globalisation' is that people have been brought closer together through global media such as the internet.

Disadvantages: to emphasise the bad or negative; for example one disadvantage of 'globalisation' is that it has eroded national identity, globally we have adopted an Americanised monoculture i.e. McDonaldisation.

Key concepts

This recap activity will ensure that you go over those all important key concepts. Complete the key concept chart by writing a definition of the concept. Refer to the core text book or your classroom notes to help you.

Key concepts	Definitions
Norms	
Values	
Status	
Roles	
Culture	
High culture	
Popular culture	
Subculture	
Cultural diversity	
Multiculturalism	
Consumer culture	
Global culture	

Mix and match

The purpose of this exercise is to test your knowledge on key concepts in socialisation, culture and identity. You will need to match up each concept with the correct definition. Each concept is numbered and the definition is lettered. Match them up by drawing a connecting line from one to the other. Then check at the bottom of the page to see if you have matched the two correctly.

1 Hidden curriculum

2 Cultural comfort zones

3 High culture

4 Role

5 Subculture

6 Socialisation

A
A term used by Tony Sewell to describe how peer groups tend to include people from very similar social backgrounds.

B
This is associated with a small elite in society who follow hobbies such as the arts, ballet, opera, polo, lacrosse, hunting and shooting.

C
The process by which individuals learn social behaviour, for example, norms and values.

D
A culture followed by a small group within society which has distinct norms and values.

E
This is responsible for teaching children the rules and regulations of school life. Norms and values are taught informally rather than being part of the formal school curriculum.

F
A pattern of behaviour; routines and responses acted out in everyday life.

Answers: 1.E, 2.A, 3.B, 4.F, 5.D, 6.C

Check your knowledge quick fire quiz

This multiple choice quiz will test your knowledge on the formation of culture and the process of socialisation. Each question is worth a number of points; the points are indicated at the end of the question. The more points a question is worth, the more difficult it is. Top mark questions reflect whether you have read your core text book thoroughly. Once you have ticked the answer you believe to be correct add up your score to reveal whether you are a sociology expert!

1 *Which of the following is NOT an agent of socialisation?* **(3 points)**

a) ☐ Education
b) ☐ Workplace
c) ☐ Political system

2 *Which of the following is a definition of the term 'culture'?* **(3 points)**

a) ☐ The way of life of a social group
b) ☐ The beliefs that everyone follows in society
c) ☐ A pattern of behaviour or routine

3 *Which of the following is not a value?* **(4 points)**

a) ☐ It is wrong to hurt others
b) ☐ It is good to be clean and hygienic
c) ☐ Be quiet in a library

4 *Which of the following is a definition of ascribed status?* **(3 points)**

a) ☐ A status which you are born into
b) ☐ A status which you get through hard work and success
c) ☐ A status which you buy

5 *Which term goes with the following definition – 'the process by which events in one part of the world come to influence what happens elsewhere in the world'?* **(3 points)**

a) ☐ Multiculturalism
b) ☐ Cultural diversity
c) ☐ Globalisation

6 *Which sociologist argues that the media are responsible for creating popular culture in the contemporary UK?* **(4 points)**

a) ☐ Strinati (1995)
b) ☐ Adorno
c) ☐ Parekh (2006)

Possible 20 points

17–20 Well done! You are definitely a sociology expert!
12–16 It's official: you are becoming a 'sociology star'!
7–11 Looks like you might be avoiding the more difficult questions – get back to reading that text book!
0–6 Oh dear: you're not going to win any 'sociology student of the year' prizes!

Answers: 1.c, 2.a, 3.c, 4.a, 5.c, 6.a

Gender identities

Key concepts

This recap activity will ensure that you go over those all important key concepts. Complete the key concept chart by writing a definition of the concept and, where relevant, include the sociologist that uses it. Refer to the core text book or your classroom notes to help you.

Key concepts	Definitions
Sex	
Gender	
Social constructionism	
Biological determinism	
Passive femininity	
Normative femininity	
Hegemonic masculinity	
Ladette	
Complicit masculinity	
Crisis of masculinity	

Mix and match

The purpose of this exercise is to test your knowledge on key pieces of sociological research on gender identities. You will need to match up each concept with the correct definition. Each concept is numbered and the definition is lettered. Match them up by drawing a connecting line from one to the other. Then check at the bottom of the page to see if you have matched the two correctly.

Concept	Definition
1 Gauntlett (2002)	A This sociologist found that the 'New Wave Girls' adopted an assertive femininity. They challenged the sexism of male teachers and their male peers in the school.
2 Sue Sharpe	B This sociologist uses the term 'hegemonic masculinity' to illustrate a masculine identity associated with male supremacy, heterosexuality, aggression and laddish culture.
3 The Lads	C This sociologist found that magazines give advice about how to be attractive in terms of gender. They teach males and females how they should dress, behave and act according to whether they are male or female.
4 Connell	D This term refers to girls who adopt more masculine behaviour such as binge drinking, swearing, smoking and being crude.
5 Ladette	E This group of boys were studied by Willis (1977). They messed around at school and thought that those boys who worked hard were feminine. They did not see qualifications as important as they planned to go and do the manual jobs that their fathers had done.
6 Blackman (1995)	F This sociologist found that girls' expectations have changed over time. In the 1970s their priorities were love and marriage, but by the 1990s this had changed to work and careers.

Answers: 1.C, 2.F, 3.E, 4.B, 5.D, 6.A

Check your knowledge quick fire quiz

This multiple choice quiz will test your knowledge on how gender identities are formed through the process of socialisation. Each question is worth a number of points; the points are indicated at the end of the question. The more points a question is worth, the more difficult it is. Top mark questions reflect whether you have read your core text book thoroughly. Once you have ticked the answer you believe to be correct, add up your score to reveal whether you are a gender identity expert!

1 *Which sociologist found that when boys talked about their parents they described their mothers as more sensitive and emotionally closer to them than their fathers?* **(4 points)**

a) ☐ Lees (1986)
b) ☐ Frosh (2002)
c) ☐ Storey (2003)

2 *Which sociologist argued that 'chick lit' persuades young women that the body is a key source of their identity?* **(3 points)**

a) ☐ Gill and Herdieckerhoff (2006)
b) ☐ Sewell (2000)
c) ☐ Sue Sharpe (1994)

3 *Which term refers to a man who is in touch with his feminine side and who takes an interest in his appearance as well as helping out with housework and childcare?* **(3 points)**

a) ☐ New Lad
b) ☐ Ladette
c) ☐ New Man

4 *Which sociologist studied young Muslim women in Coventry and Bradford and found that although their religion was important to them they wanted to move beyond traditional roles and pursue higher education and careers?* **(4 points)**

a) ☐ Butler (1995)
b) ☐ Modood (2005)
c) ☐ Jacobson (1997)

5 *Which of the following is NOT a type of masculinity identified by Connell (2002)?* **(3 points)**

a) ☐ Complicit
b) ☐ Marginalised
c) ☐ Assertive

6 *Which sociologist found that some Asian footballers tried to hide aspects of their Asian identity in order to fit in with the laddish behaviour of the other players?* **(3 points)**

a) ☐ Burdsey (2004)
b) ☐ Sharpe (1994)
c) ☐ Willis (1977)

Possible 20 points

17–20 Well done! You are definitely a gender identity expert!
12–16 It's official: you are becoming a 'sociology star'!
7–11 Looks like you might be avoiding the more difficult questions – get back to reading that text book!
0–6 Oh dear: you're not going to win any 'sociology student of the year' prizes!

Answers: 1.b, 2.a, 3.c, 4.a, 5.c, 6.a

Social class identities

Key concepts

This recap activity will ensure that you go over those all important key concepts. Complete the key concept chart by writing a definition of the concept and, where possible, include which sociologist uses it. Refer to your core text book or your classroom notes.

Key concepts	Definitions
Social class	
Capitalism	
Life chances	
Status	
Class conflict	
Bourgeoisie	
Proletariat	
Economic capital	
Cultural capital	
Social capital	
Conspicuous consumption	
NS-Sec model	
Lifestyle (postmodern)	
Ascribed status	
Achieved status	

Mix and match

The purpose of this exercise is to get you to test your knowledge on key pieces of sociological research on social class identities. You will need to match the explanation of the research/theory with the title of the study. Each sociologist/ title of study is numbered and the explanation of the study is lettered. Match the correct research with the title of the study by drawing a connecting line from one to the other. Then check at the bottom of the page to see if you have matched the two correctly.

1
Class consciousness

2
'Resources'

3
Consumer culture

4
Skeggs (1997)

5
Lifestyle and employment

6
'Super-rich'

A
Postmodernists argue that due to this change in culture, individuals are able to 'pick and mix' their identity.

B
This sociologist found that the working class women in her study tried to distance themselves from the norms and values of traditional working class women.

C
This term was used by Karl Marx in his description of how the working class would become aware of their exploitation by the ruling class.

D
Savage (1992) identified a split in the middle classes. The split was based on these two things.

E
This group are a sub-group of the upper class; those in this group have generally achieved their status.

F
Pierre Bourdieu, a neo-Marxist supporter, used the concept of 'capital' to illustrate social class differences. This word describes what 'economic capital' means.

Answers: 1.C, 2.F, 3.A, 4.B, 5.D, 6.E.

Check your knowledge quick fire quiz

This multiple choice quiz will test your knowledge on how social class identities are formed through the process of socialisation. Each question is worth a number of points; the points are indicated at the end of the question. The more points a question is worth, the more difficult it is. Top mark questions reflect whether you have read your core text book thoroughly. Once you have ticked the answer you believe to be correct, add up your score to reveal whether you are a social class identity expert!

1 *Whose research on 'planned teenage pregnancy' found that the family of the pregnant teenager was a great influence on the decision making process of the teenager?* **(4 points)**

a) ☐ Cater and Coleman (2006)
b) ☐ Power et al (2003)
c) ☐ Medhurst (1999)

2 *Whose research found that there was a close relationship between children from middle class backgrounds who had attended public schools and those that got places at elite universities?* **(3 points)**

a) ☐ Power et al (2003)
b) ☐ Reay (1998)
c) ☐ Karl Marx

3 *Brundson (1997) found that middle class homes went without a form of media technology as they perceived the form of media as a tasteless, inferior form of working class culture. What was the form of media technology?* **(3 points)**

a) ☐ Mp3 player
b) ☐ Mobile phone
c) ☐ Satellite TV

4 *Which religion is likely to have a working class base, as it is normally found in inner city communities?* **(3 points)**

a) ☐ Christianity
b) ☐ Rastafarianism
c) ☐ Islam

5 *Whose research on a group of white skinheads found that working class identity was important and that the skinheads worked hard at constructing a culture of 'whiteness'?* **(4 points)**

a) ☐ Willis (1977)
b) ☐ Brah (1999)
c) ☐ Savage (1992)

6 *In 2005 Savage's study in Cheadle, Manchester, found a strong culture of manual labour, which gave the area a feeling of what?* **(3 points)**

a) ☐ 'Practical structure'
b) ☐ 'Practical flavour'
c) ☐ 'Practical culture'

Possible 20 points

17–20 Well done! You are definitely a social class identity expert!
12–16 It's official: you are becoming a 'sociology star'!
7–11 Looks like you might be avoiding the more difficult questions – get back to reading that text book!
0–6 Oh dear: you're not going to win any 'sociology student of the year' prizes!

Answers: 1.a, 2.a, 3.c, 4.b, 5.b, 6.b

Ethnic identities

Key concepts 

This recap activity will ensure that you go over those all important key concepts. Complete the key concept chart by writing a definition of the concept and, where possible, include which sociologist uses it. Refer to your core text book or your classroom notes.

Key concepts	Definitions
Race	
Ethnicity	
Nationality	
Ethnic minority group	
Immigrant	
Immigrant hosts	
Hybridity	
Little Englanders	
Globalisation	
Assimilation	
Cultural diversity	
Code switching	

Mix and match

The purpose of this exercise is to get you to test your knowledge on key pieces of sociological research on ethnic identities. You will need to match the explanation of the research/theory with the title of the study. Each sociologist/title of study is numbered and the explanation of the study is lettered. Match the correct research with the title of the study by drawing a connecting line from one to the other. Then check at the bottom of the page to see if you have matched the two correctly.

Number	Sociologist/title of study
1	Hewitt (1996)
2	'Othering'
3	Bond and Rosie (2006)
4	Assimilation
5	'Dual identities'
6	Globalisation

Letter	Explanation
A	This process involves individuals seeing themselves as positive and anything different from them as negative.
B	This sociologist argued that his research showed that the young white working class in the UK felt a sense of injustice as they felt they could not celebrate their white working class culture.
C	This term is used to explain the process by which the various countries and cultures of the world become more closely intertwined.
D	This term was used by Johal and Bains (1998) to describe how second and third generation immigrants have a number of different identities, which they switch to depending on who they are with.
E	These sociologists found in their research amongst Scottish people that, in terms of identity, they identified themselves by their ethnic identity as Scottish over their national identity as British.
F	This concept explains the process that takes place when immigrants to the UK abandon their homeland culture in favour of British culture.

Answers: 1.B, 2.A, 3.E, 4.F, 5.D, 6.C

Check your knowledge quick fire quiz

This multiple choice quiz will test your knowledge on how ethnic identities are formed through the process of socialisation. Each question is worth a number of points; the points are indicated at the end of the question. The more points a question is worth, the more difficult it is. Top mark questions reflect whether you have read your core text book thoroughly. Once you have ticked the answer you believe to be correct, add up your score to reveal whether you are an ethnic identity expert!

1 *Which sociologist found that, for Bangladeshi families, the extended family was still important?* **(4 points)**

a) ☐ Modood (1997)
b) ☐ Mason (2005)
c) ☐ Dench et al (2006)

2 *Which sociologist argued that the national curriculum needs to be more inclusive of Black history, and that positive achievements in Black history need to be emphasised?* **(3 points)**

a) ☐ Wright (2006)
b) ☐ Sewell (2000)
c) ☐ Derrington and Kendall (2004)

3 *Modood (2005) observed that 100 years ago the African American theorist Du Bois argued that the 20th century would be the century of colour (divided between black & white). In the 21st century what is the divide characterised by?* **(3 points)**

a) ☐ Islam and the West
b) ☐ Protestant and Catholic
c) ☐ Black and White

4 *What is the term used to describe how peers from the same ethnic group form friendships and socialise together because they feel a sense of 'sameness'?* **(3 points)**

a) ☐ Ethnic zone
b) ☐ Cultural comfort zone
c) ☐ Code switching

5 *Whose research found that, in the 1970s and into the late 1990s, ethnic representation in the media was limited to stereotypes and marginalisation?* **(4 points)**

a) ☐ Modood (1997)
b) ☐ Song (2003)
c) ☐ Jhally (1992)

6 *In 2003, Song found that many Chinese living in the UK were employed in the food and catering sector, mainly in Chinese take-aways and restaurants. Song argued that an agent of socialisation was important in influencing employment. What was the agent Song referred to?* **(3 points)**

a) ☐ Family
b) ☐ Education
c) ☐ Peers

Possible 20 points

17–20 Well done! You are definitely an ethnic identity expert!
12–16 It's official: you are becoming a 'sociology star'!
7–11 Looks like you might be avoiding the more difficult questions – get back to reading that text book!
0–6 Oh dear: you're not going to win any 'sociology student of the year' prizes!

Answers: 1.c, 2.b, 3.a, 4.b, 5.c, 6.a

Age identities

Key concepts

This recap activity will ensure that you go over those all important key concepts. Complete the key concept chart by writing a definition of the concept and, where possible, include which sociologist uses it. Refer to your core text book or your classroom notes.

Key concepts	Definitions
Age	
Youth	
Middle age	
Old age	
Supermarket of style	
Oldest old	
Sub-culture	
Life course	
Active ageing	
First age (Laslett 1991)	
Second age (Laslett 1991)	
Third age (Laslett 1991)	

Mix and match

revise

The purpose of this exercise is to get you to test your knowledge on key pieces of sociological research on age identity. You will need to match the explanation of the research/theory with the title of the study. Each sociologist/title of study is numbered and the explanation of the study is lettered. Match the correct research with the title of the study by drawing a connecting line from one to the other. Then check at the bottom of the page to see if you have matched the two correctly.

1
Abrams (1959)

2
Postmodern

3
Victor (2005)

4
Bradley (1996)

5
Bytheway (2005)

6
'Active ageing'

A
This sociologist argued that, although people accept chronological ageing, they have difficulty fitting themselves into the two categories of middle and old age.

B
This sociologist argued that middle age can bring with it a higher status than being young or old.

C
This concept was used in the study by Clarke and Warren (2007) who argued that those they studied between the ages of 60 and 96 engaged with old age in a positive, pro-active way.

D
This perspective identified youth culture as a time for experimenting, a time to pick and mix symbols and styles, in order to create different identities.

E
This sociologist argues that middle age is a distinctive phase of life, related to people in their forties and fifties before they reach the period of old age.

F
This sociologist argued that young people are all part of the same youth culture, and this is known as the transitional stage.

Answers: 1.F, 2.D, 3.E, 4.B, 5.A, 6.C

Check your knowledge quick fire quiz

This multiple choice quiz will test your knowledge on how age identity is formed through the process of socialisation. Each question is worth a number of points; the points are indicated at the end of the question. The more points a question is worth, the more difficult it is. Top mark questions reflect whether you have read your core text book thoroughly. Once you have ticked the answer you believe to be correct, add up your score to reveal whether you are an age identity expert!

1 *In education, the words used by teachers, such as 'young' or 'old', can in some way reinforce age identity. What do sociologists call this process?* (**4 points)**

a) ☐ The hidden curriculum
b) ☐ The historical curriculum
c) ☐ The national curriculum

2 *What agent of socialisation is particularly important in shaping youth identity?* **(3 points)**

a) ☐ Religion
b) ☐ Workplace
c) ☐ Peers

3 *Whose research on Asian girls found that the girls formed distinct identities as a way of coping with school?* **(3 points)**

a) ☐ McKingsley (2001)
b) ☐ Shain (2003)
c) ☐ Bradley (1996)

4 *Who argued that religion was used as a coping strategy for those 85 and over?* **(3 points)**

a) ☐ Polemus (1997)
b) ☐ McKingsley (2001)
c) ☐ Clarke (1976)

5 *Muncie's (2004) study of the media found that youth were represented in a marginalised way. How were they represented?* **(4 points)**

a) ☐ Cheeky and bright
b) ☐ Creative and risk taking
c) ☐ Deviant and troublesome

6 *What is the most likely site for age discrimination in the UK?* **(3 points)**

a) ☐ Classroom
b) ☐ Home
c) ☐ Workplace

Possible 20 points

17–20 Well done! You are definitely an age identity expert!
12–16 It's official: you are becoming a 'sociology star'!
7–11 Looks like you might be avoiding the more difficult questions – get back to reading that text book!
0–6 Oh dear: you're not going to win any 'sociology student of the year' prizes!

Answers: 1.a, 2.c, 3.b, 4.b, 5.c, 6.c

Research methods

Revision checklist

The list below outlines all the topics and sub topics which you need to cover in your revision. The points referred to below can all be found in the core text book.

Exploring the research process

Key concepts:

- Validity ☐
- Reliability ☐
- Representativeness ☐
- Generalisability ☐

Key stages in the research process

- Research questions ☐
- Operationalisation ☐
- Primary methods ☐
- Secondary methods ☐
- Sampling ☐
- Access ☐
- Ethics ☐
- Pilot studies ☐
- Interpretation of data ☐

Use of quantitative data-collection methods and analysis in the context of research

Quantitative methods (strengths, weaknesses and suitability for various research topics):

- Questionnaires ☐
- Structured interviews ☐
- Statistical data ☐
- Content analysis ☐

Key concepts:

- Patterns ☐
- Trends ☐
- Cause and effect ☐
- Positivism ☐
- Reliability ☐
- Objectivity ☐
- Value freedom ☐
- Quantitative data analysis ☐

Exploring the use of qualitative data collection methods in the context of research

Qualitative methods (strengths, weaknesses and suitability for various research topics):

- Observation ☐
- Unstructured interviews ☐
- Semi-structured interviews ☐
- Personal documents ☐
- Ethnography ☐
- Focus group interviews ☐

Key concepts:

- Meanings and experiences ☐
- Interpretivism ☐
- Verstehen ☐
- Validity ☐
- Empathy ☐
- Rapport ☐
- Qualitative data analysis ☐

Exploring the use of mixed methods in the context of research

Key concepts:

- Triangulation ☐
- Methodological pluralism ☐
- Fitness for purpose ☐
- Mixed methods data analysis ☐

Key concepts

This recap activity will ensure that you go over those all important key concepts. Complete the key concept chart by writing a definition of the concept in the space provided. Refer to your core text book or your classroom notes.

Key concepts	Definitions
Quantitative	
Qualitative	
Positivism	
Interpretivism	
Validity	
Reliability	
Representativeness	
Generalisability	
Primary research	
Secondary research	
Operationalisation	
Methodological pluralism	
Triangulation	

Mix and match 

The purpose of this exercise is to test your knowledge on the strengths and weaknesses of different research methods. You will need to match up each description of a strength or weakness with the correct method. Each method is numbered and the strengths/weaknesses are lettered. Match them up by drawing a connecting line from one to the other. Then check at the bottom of the page to see if you have matched the two correctly.

1 Postal questionnaire

2 Official statistics

3 Focus group interviews

4 Content analysis

5 Unstructured interview

6 Covert participant observation

A This method is viewed as being unethical as it is not possible to gain informed consent from participants.

B This method is seen as being highly valid as respondents are free to go into as much detail as they wish and therefore rich and in-depth data can be gathered.

C This method is appealing as the data is already gathered and often based on large representative samples.

D This method has a low response rate as people often do not return them.

E This method generates large amounts of data in a short time and the interaction between respondents can increase the validity of the findings.

F This is a systematic way of analysing media content and therefore produces quantitative data high in reliability.

Answers: 1.D, 2.C, 3.E, 4.F, 5.B, 6.A

Application task

Look at the research methods listed below. For each one note down in the blank columns whether the method is primary or secondary and whether it is quantitative or qualitative. The first one has been done for you.

Method	Primary or Secondary?	Quantitative or Qualitative?
1. Questionnaire	Primary	Quantitative
2. Unstructured interview		
3. Content analysis		
4. Covert participant observation		
5. Semi-structured interview		
6. Official statistics		
7. Overt structured observation		
8. Structured interview		

Answers: 1. Primary and Quantitative, 2. Primary and Qualitative,
3. Secondary and Quantitative, 4. Primary and Qualitative,
5. Primary and Quantitative and Qualitative, 6. Secondary and Quantitative,
7. Primary and Quantitative and Qualitative, 8. Primary and Quantitative

ExamCafé

Gender identities

Part (a) questions

This part of the question assesses your knowledge and understanding (AO1) of a concept. In order to write a good answer you will need to:

- write a clear definition of what the concept means
- demonstrate that you understand the question through giving examples.

Examples can be taken from the pre release material or elsewhere. You should spend approximately 5 minutes on this part of the question. It is worth 8 AO1 marks.

Good example

The following answer is a very strong one and covers all the points mentioned above. Read the answer and highlight where the candidate has given the definition and examples which illustrate it.

(a) Define the concept of 'norms'. (8 marks)

Student answer

A norm is a form of behaviour which most people in society follow. Norms are unwritten rules which guide human behaviour. Individuals learn norms through socialisation and the first norms they learn are through primary socialisation from their parents. Examples of such norms include eating food with a knife and fork, washing hands before dinner, and sitting down to eat. Other norms are often learnt through secondary socialisation. For example, when a child begins school they learn further norms such as they should wear uniform, be quiet when the teacher is talking and to attend on time.

Example to improve

The example below could be improved. Using the guidance above try to identify what this answer does not do. Then rewrite the answer trying to cover all the points in the checklist.

(a) Define the concept of 'values'. (8 marks)

Student answer

Values are things like thinking that you should not hurt others or steal from them.

Now try your own

Now try to write an answer to the question below. Remember to use the guidance above. Ask your teacher to check your answer if you wish.

(a) Define the concept of 'roles'. (8 marks)

Part (b) questions

This part of the question assesses your knowledge and understanding (AO1) and your interpretation and application (AO2a) of sociological ideas. It is worth 16 marks: 12 marks for AO1 and 4 marks for AO2a. You should:

- refer to concepts, research studies, examples and, if relevant, theory
- write two clear paragraphs – one for each point and should refer to at least one piece of sociological research in each.

You should spend approximately 15 minutes on part (b).

Good example

The following answer is a very strong one and covers all the points mentioned above. Read the answer and highlight where the candidate has referred to a key concept, research study or example.

(b) Outline and explain how any two agents of socialisation influence femininities. (16 marks)

Student answer

One agent of socialisation which influences femininities is the family. Families teach females what they regard to be appropriate feminine behaviour. For example, in Asian families femininity is often viewed in a traditional way seeing the female role as that of wife and mother. Seidler (2006) found that girls from some Asian backgrounds learn that they should behave differently to their brothers and have less freedom. Anne Oakley found that families also teach girls to be interested in traditionally female pursuits such as cooking and looking after children. They do this by giving girls toys such as dolls and cookers and encouraging them to play games such as 'mummies and daddies'.

Another agent of socialisation which may influence femininities is the mass media. The mass media teaches females how to behave and dress in accordance with their gender. Gauntlett (2002) claims that magazines give advice to women about how to be attractive in a feminine way. They use celebrity role models such as Kate Moss to illustrate this. Gill and Herdieckerhoff (2006) argue that 'chick lit' books teach young women that in order to be feminine you should have a sexy body. Such books also highlight the idea that to be feminine is to be vulnerable as often the females in these stories need to be rescued by male characters.

Example to improve

The example below could be improved. Using the guidance above try to identify what this answer does not do. Then rewrite the answer trying to cover all the points in the checklist.

(b) Outline and explain how any two agents of socialisation may influence masculine identities. (16 marks)

Student answer

One agent of socialisation which influences masculine identities is the peer group. Burdsey found that young Asian footballers would often hide their ethnic identity in order to act in a more laddish and masculine way with their peers.

Another agent of socialisation which influences masculine identities is education.

Some boys do not work hard at school because they do not think it is masculine. They may be afraid of being bullied by others and therefore do not study.

Now try your own

Now try to write an answer to the question below. Remember to use the guidance above. Ask your teacher to check your answer if you wish.

(b) Outline and explain how any two agents of socialisation may influence gender identities. (16 marks)

Part (c) questions

This part of the question assesses your knowledge and understanding (AO1), your interpretation and application skills (AO2a) and your analysis and evaluation skills (AO2b). It is worth 24 marks: 12 marks for AO1, 8 marks for AO2a and 4 marks for AO2b. You should:

- refer to concepts, research studies, examples and, if relevant, theory
- make some evaluative points.

You should spend approximately 20 minutes on part (c).

Good example

The following answer is a strong one and covers all the points mentioned above. Read the answer and highlight where the candidate has referred to a key concept, research study, example or made an evaluative point.

(c) Explain and briefly evaluate why male gender identities may have changed in the contemporary UK. (24 marks)

Student answer

Male gender identities have been traditionally viewed as 'hegemonic'. This term was used by Connell and is associated with male power and dominance, heterosexuality, aggression and laddishness. This type of masculine identity was often seen in men who did traditionally working class manual jobs. For example, Nayak (2006) argues that in the 1950s and 1960s men had 'body capital' which means they did hard physical work and were the main breadwinner. Willis (1977) also found that the 'lads' in his study associated masculinity with manual labour. They viewed schoolwork as feminine as it was not needed in order for them to do the same manual jobs their fathers did. However, Willis's study was only based on a small sample of twelve boys and therefore the findings are not generalisable. It is argued by sociologists that due to the decline in manual employment in the UK there is less evidence of hegemonic masculine identities. Mac and Ghaill argue that there has been a 'crisis of masculinity' with men feeling that their masculinity has been threatened as their jobs have been taken away. Connell uses the term 'marginalised masculinity' to describe this.

The media may also have played a part in the change in masculine identities. The media began to represent man in different ways by advertising beauty, grooming and fashion products to them. Nixon argues that the 'new man' identity was created by the media and advertising. The 'new man' is a man who is in touch with his feminine side, who takes care of his appearance and who helps out with housework and childcare. Connell uses the term 'complicit masculinity' to describe the behaviour of the 'new man'.

Another reason that masculine identities may have changed is that it has become more acceptable to be homosexual. This is evidenced by the introduction of the civil partnership for gay couples in 2004. There is now more evidence of gay male identities and also of metrosexual ones. 'Metrosexuals' are those men who are heterosexual but present themselves in what is regarded as an effeminate and possibly homosexual manner; for example, David Beckham.

However, although there is evidence that masculine identities have changed and new ones have emerged, the extent to which this has happened and the reasons why may vary according to the class, ethnicity, age and geographical location of the men concerned. There may be regional differences depending on the type of employment available in different areas.

Example to improve

The example below could be improved. Using the guidance above try to identify what this answer does not do. Then rewrite the answer trying to cover all the points in the checklist.

(c) Explain and briefly evaluate the ways in which female identities are created and reinforced in the contemporary UK. (24 marks)

Student answer

One way in which female gender identities are created is through religion. Religion teaches females behaviours and expectations. For example, in Muslim culture 'izzat' (family honour) teaches females that in order to be good daughters they should marry, raise children and not bring any shame upon the family.

Another way female identities are created is through the media. Girls' magazines teach girls to be interested in boys and fashion and their appearance. They have celebrity role models which girls want to copy. However, there are a range of magazines available for young women and they do not all give the same messages.

Another way in which female gender identities are created is through the family. Parents dress girls in pink and give them toys such as dolls and replica kitchen sets.

They may also try to protect girls more than they do boys by not letting them out.

Education may also create female gender identities. Some sociologists argue that girls are directed towards certain subjects by teachers. They are more likely to choose hairdressing or health and social care.

Now try your own

Now try to write an answer to the question below. Remember to use the guidance above. Ask your teacher to check your answer if you wish.

(c) Outline and briefly evaluate the ways in which masculine identities are created and reinforced in the contemporary UK. (24 points)

ExamCafé

Social class identities

Part (a) questions

This part of the question assesses your knowledge and understanding (AO1) of a concept. In order to write a good answer you will need to:

- write a clear definition of what the concept means
- demonstrate that you understand the question through giving examples.

Examples can be taken from the pre release material or elsewhere. You should spend approximately 5 minutes on this part of the question. It is worth 8 AO1 marks.

Good example

The following answer is a very strong one and covers all the points mentioned above. Read the answer and highlight where the candidate has given the definition and examples which illustrate it.

(a) Define the concept of 'super rich'. (8 marks)

Student answer

The 'super rich' are a sub group within the upper class. These people have achieved their wealth and status through hard work and merit. These people are often associated with having a glamorous lifestyle and demonstrating conspicuous consumption. Examples of the super rich are celebrities such as the Beckhams and entrepreneurs such as Richard Branson. They value material consumer goods and brand names and live a visibly rich lifestyle. This group often gain status and social capital through networking with other super rich people. For example, the Beckhams are often seen at social events with Tom Cruise and his wife. The super rich are sometimes looked down upon by other members of the upper class who have inherited their status and see the super rich as having little class and poor breeding.

Example to improve

The example below could be improved. Using the guidance above try to identify what this answer does not do. Then rewrite the answer trying to cover all the points in the checklist.

(a) Define the concept of 'high culture'. (8 marks)

Student answer

High culture is linked to those in the upper class. It is to do with liking polo, opera, ballet and blood sports.

Now try your own

Now try to write an answer to the question below. Remember to use the guidance above. Ask your teacher to check your answer if you wish.

(a) Define the concept of 'popular culture'. (8 marks)

Part (b) questions

This part of the question assesses your knowledge and understanding (AO1) and your interpretation and application (AO2a) of sociological ideas. It is worth 16 marks: 12 marks for AO1 and 4 marks for AO2a. You should:

- refer to concepts, research studies, examples and, if relevant, theory
- write two clear paragraphs – one for each point and should refer to at least one piece of sociological research in each.

You should spend approximately 15 minutes on part (b).

Good example

The following answer is a very strong one and covers all the points mentioned above. Read the answer and highlight where the candidate has referred to a key concept, research study or example.

(b) Outline and explain two ways in which middle class identity is formed. (16 marks)

Student answer

One way in which middle class identity is formed is through family. The middle class family is seen to be more child centred and concerned about their child's education than working class families. Reay (1998) found that middle class mothers influenced their child's primary schooling more than working class mothers. Middle class parents are also thought to give their children an advantage by giving them 'cultural capital'. Cultural capital refers to a knowledge of the arts which is required in certain social circles or situations. For example, knowing about classical music, theatre, art and foreign countries. This may help them in education and also when attending interviews or networking.

Another way in which middle class identity is formed is through education. Middle class children achieve more highly than working class children. It has been argued that this is because they have an advantage at school because teachers are also middle class and therefore perceive middle class children as being more intelligent. Bernstein argued that this is because middle class children speak using an elaborate language code, like teachers do, and the working class use a restricted code. Teachers encourage the middle class children more because of this. Power et al (2003) found that middle class children were much more likely to attend the elite universities.

Example to improve

The example below could be improved. Using the guidance above try to identify what this answer does not do. Then rewrite the answer trying to cover all the points in the checklist.

(b) Outline and explain two ways in which working class identity is formed. (16 marks)

Student answer

One way in which working class identity is formed is through work. The male working class often base their identities around their manual jobs. They form strong links with their co-workers and tend to have an 'us and them' relationship with their bosses. Their jobs are often based on masculine traits such as toughness and physical strength.

Another way working class identity is formed is through the family. The working class family is often extended and has a strong sense of family loyalty. The roles within the working class family are often more traditional with a male breadwinner and a female housewife.

Now try your own

Now try to write an answer to the question below. Remember to use the guidance above. Ask your teacher to check your answer if you wish.

(b) Outline and explain two ways in which upper class identity is formed. (16 marks)

Part (c) questions

This part of the question assesses your knowledge and understanding (AO1), your interpretation and application skills (AO2a) and your analysis and evaluation skills (AO2b). It is worth 24 marks: 12 marks for AO1, 8 marks for AO2a and 4 marks for AO2b. You should:

- refer to concepts, research studies, examples and, if relevant, theory
- make some evaluative points.

You should spend approximately 20 minutes on part (c).

Good example

The following answer is a strong one and covers all the points mentioned above. Read the answer and highlight where the candidate has referred to a key concept, research study, example or made an evaluative point.

(c) Explain and briefly evaluate the view that education is the most important agent in shaping social class identity. (24 marks)

Student answer

There is evidence that education is the most important agent in shaping social class identity. This is because how well children do in education will determine what qualifications they get and what life chances they will have. The middle class tend to achieve more highly in education than the working class. Bourdieu argues that this is because their parents socialise them into having cultural capital. This means they take them to the theatre, museums, art galleries and on foreign holidays. There is also evidence that middle class parents are more focussed on their children's education than working class parents. Douglas found that middle class parents were more likely to attend parents' evenings than working class parents. However, this may not be because they were less interested but because they face more pressures in terms of having to work longer hours and not being granted time off.

Nevertheless, other agents of socialisation may be as important as education in shaping social class identity. The media represents each social class differently. For example, in programmes such as Shameless the working class are shown as aggressive, assertive and good at playing the social security system. Medhurst (1999) showed how a group of middle class students watching The Royle Family believed it was an accurate portrayal of working class life in the UK. Also, different types of media are directed at different social classes and this can reinforce their identities. For example, broadsheet newspapers such as The Times and the Guardian are associated with the middle classes whereas tabloid newspapers are associated with the working classes. These newspapers are written in different styles and feature different types of articles. Tabloid newspapers are more likely to focus on popular culture items such as celebrities and sport whereas the broadsheets focus on more detailed news coverage and types of entertainment such as the Arts.

The peer group could also be an important agent in shaping working class identity. Willis (1977) found that the 'lads' in his study had a strong peer culture which stressed the importance of masculine behaviour and aspiring to do working class manual jobs. However, Willis only studied 12 lads and therefore his findings cannot be generalised. Brah (1999) found that for the white skinheads he studied the peer group was important in creating a strong sense of working class identity.

Example to improve

The example below could be improved. Using the guidance above try to identify what this answer does not do. Then rewrite the answer trying to cover all the points in the checklist.

(c) Explain and briefly evaluate the ways in which social class identities are created and reinforced in the contemporary UK. (24 marks)

Student answer

Children automatically take on the same social class as their parents until they get jobs of their own. The parents' social class background may affect how they bring up their children.

Willis argued that working class identities are developed through the peer group. He studied the lads and found that they had a masculine peer group culture which emphasised toughness and aggression.

Bourdieu argues that the middle class have 'cultural capital'. They take children to museums, art galleries and foreign holidays and this gives them an advantage in education.

Medhurst found that a group of middle class students watching The Royle Family believed it was an accurate portrayal of working class life in the contemporary UK.

Savage claims that for a group of middle class doctors in Cheadle, their occupation was the key source of their identity.

Now try your own

Now try to write an answer to the question below. Remember to use the guidance above. Ask your teacher to check your answer if you wish.

(c) Explain and briefly evaluate the ways in which class identity may have changed in the contemporary UK. (24 marks)

Exam**Café**

Ethnic identities

Part (a) questions

This part of the question assesses your knowledge and understanding (AO1) of a concept. In order to write a good answer you will need to:

- write a clear definition of what the concept means
- demonstrate that you understand the question through giving examples.

Examples can be taken from the pre release material or elsewhere. You should spend approximately 5 minutes on this part of the question. It is worth 8 AO1 marks.

Good example

The following answer is a very strong one and covers all the points mentioned above. Read the answer and highlight where the candidate has given the definition and examples which illustrate it.

(a) Define the concept of hybridity. (8 marks)

Student answer

Hybridity is the term used to describe a mix of two or more cultural influences in the creation of one identity. Les Back's research on a council estate in London revealed that hybrid cultural identities were not fixed but were created by young people who 'played with different cultural masks'. For example the 'Wigger' hybrid identity is created by white youths mixing African American 'gangsta' culture with their British identity. Through the use of cultural artefacts such as music, dress and symbols, an individual can shape their own hybrid identity. Another example of hybridity was found by Johal. His research showed that young Asian males took part in what he called 'code-switching' in which the young males changed their identity and behaviour depending on who they were with i.e. friends or family.

Example to improve

The example below could be improved. Using the guidance above try to identify what this answer does not do. Then rewrite the answer trying to cover all the points in the checklist.

(a) Define the concept of 'multiculturalism'. (8 marks)

Student answer

Multiculturalism is when there is more than one culture present in a society. It is the promotion of all cultures having equal rights and that their beliefs should be seen as equal, meaning that they have the same status. This is one way to define it as there is much debate amongst sociologists as to the precise definition of the term. An example of multiculturalism is evident in the school curriculum; now all children are taught about different religions, this encourages tolerance and acceptance. Also the media promotes multiculturalism; the BBC has an Asian radio station and they play highlights on the radio from the West Indian based Notting Hill Carnival.

Now try your own

Now try to write an answer to the question below. Remember to use the guidance above. Ask your teacher to check your answer if you wish.

(a) Define the concept of ethnic identities. (8 marks)

Part (b) questions

This part of the question assesses your knowledge and understanding (AO1) and your interpretation and application (AO2a) of sociological ideas. It is worth 16 marks: 12 marks for AO1 and 4 marks for AO2a. You should:

- refer to concepts, research studies, examples and, if relevant, theory
- write two clear paragraphs – one for each point and should refer to at least one piece of sociological research in each.

You should spend approximately 15 minutes on part (b).

Good example

The following answer is a very strong one and covers all the points mentioned above. Read the answer and highlight where the candidate has referred to a concept, research study or example.

(b) Outline and explain two ways in which ethnic identities are created and reinforced. (16 marks)

Student answer

Ethnic identities are created and reinforced by both primary and secondary socialisation. The family is the most important agent of primary socialisation; this is when an individual first learns about their ethnic heritage. Modood (2005) describes this process as the first time we become aware of our ethnic culture through food, language, dress, rituals and traditions. Miri Song's study on British Chinese found that Chinese parents were very influential in reinforcing Chinese values by positively sanctioning children who choose to help out in the family business. These children were seen as more 'Chinese' as they adopted the Chinese cultural characteristics of family solidarity and collective loyalty.

Another way in which ethnic identities are created and reinforced is through the secondary agent of socialisation, religion. Religion can also be considered as a primary agent of socialisation as many ethnic cultures are heavily influenced by religion; these beliefs are passed down through the family from generation to generation. Charlotte Butler in her 1995 study of Muslim girls found that their religion was central to creating their ethnic identity. Butler found that the teachings of Islam were a real guide in the girls' lives. However Butler did find that although religion was a major source of socialisation, the girls' peers were also an influence on their ethnic and gender identity, and the British influence from their friends in conjunction with Islam gave the girls choice and freedom in expressing their identity.

Example to improve

The example below could be improved. Using the guidance above try to identify what this answer does not do. Then rewrite the answer trying to cover all the points in the checklist.

(b) Outline and explain two ways in which secondary agents of socialisation create hybrid identities. (16 marks)

Student answer

One way in which secondary agents of socialisation create hybrid identities is through education; children at school mix with others from different cultural backgrounds, and these influences create hybrid identities. A sociologist found that at school Asian boys would take on a dual identity and live up to the expectations of their British peers. The Asian boys downplayed their ethnic identity and exaggerated their national identity. Schools and colleges promote cultural diversity and encourage the idea that Britain is a 'multicultural' society through providing cuisine from around the world; this enables pupils to mix and match their culture through consuming food that has different cultural influences. Schools also encourage students to see the value of other cultures by putting on events such as 'Black History Month' and having celebrations for religious festivals and events such as Christmas and Eid.

Another way is through the media. The media show us that we can pick and mix our identity and create our own hybrid identity; this is evident in music, films and on television shows. The media has been influential in creating hybrid identities, particularly when it comes to language; for example the famous terms 'bling' and 'booyakasha' (meaning hello) of comedy character 'Ali G' have become part of everyday language for many young people.

Now try your own

Now try to write an answer to the question below. Remember to use the guidance above. Ask your teacher to check your answer if you wish.

(b) Outline and explain two ways in which new ethnic identities are created and reinforced. (16 marks)

Part (c) questions

This part of the question assesses your knowledge and understanding (AO1), your interpretation and application skills (AO2a) and your analysis and evaluation skills (AO2b). It is worth 24 marks: 12 marks for AO1, and 8 marks for AO2a, and 4 marks for AO2b. You should:

- refer to concepts, research studies, examples and, if relevant, theory
- make some evaluative points.

You should spend approximately 20 minutes on part (c).

The following answer is a very strong one and covers all the points mentioned above. Read the answer and highlight where the candidate has referred to a concept, research study, example or made an evaluative point.

(c) Outline and briefly evaluate the view that peer groups are responsible for the creation of ethnic hybrids in the contemporary UK. (24 Marks)

Student answer

This essay will consider the view that peer groups are responsible for creating hybrid identities in the UK. Hybrid identities are created through the mixing of more that one cultural influence in order to create a whole new individual identity. Hybrid identities are formed and reinforced by the primary and secondary agents of socialisation. The peer group is one of the secondary agents of socialisation and is argued as being one of the most influential agents in creating hybrid identities. Johal (1998) found in his study of second and third generation that British Asians had a dual identity; they inherited their Asian identity from their family, and created a British identity in order to fit in with white peers at school or college. Johal called this the 'white mask' and argued that British Asian had to go through 'code-switching' between their Asian identity and their British identity to ensure that they would be accepted by their white peers. Les Back's (1996) study found that young people played with different cultural styles and that peers were particularly influential in adopting different cultural masks and creating cultural identities. Back found that new hybrid identities were emerging amongst young people in council estates; groups of white, Asian and black peers experimented with different styles, meanings and symbols borrowed from different cultures. Back concluded by stating that the hybrid identities created by the young people were breaking down inter-racial conflict and divisive lines between ethnic groups.

However, it could be argued that the media is a more important agent of socialisation in the creation of hybrid identities. Global media forms such as television, music and the Internet have introduced British society to different cultures and the process of globalisation has allowed individuals to adopt different cultures. Music as one form of media has promoted hybridity; this is evident in the music by such artists as MC Panjabi whose music is a fusion of bhangra and hip hop. Brasian music for the first time had a stage at the 2004 Glastonbury festival (Waugh et al, 2008), this was a positive step in promoting Brasian culture and hybrid identity.

In conclusion, although the peer group is influential in creating hybrid identities through the sharing of cultural 'masks', the media is active in promoting different types of culture including global culture through media forms such as the Internet. Furthermore, the other agents of primary and secondary socialisation such as family and religion are also influential in creating hybrid identities.

Example to improve

The example below could be improved. Using the guidance above try to identify what this answer does not do. Then rewrite the answer trying to cover all the points in the checklist.

(c) Outline and briefly evaluate the view that education reinforces ethnic identity. (24 marks)

Student answer

Education is a secondary agent of socialisation and has been used to reinforce ethnic identity. A study by a sociologist found that schools are ethnocentric and that British culture is seen as superior. This can have a negative effect on Asian and black pupils as they feel inferior and they have to wear a 'white mask' in order to fit in. Black and Asian children experience discrimination at school due to the informal and formal curriculum. Mason argues that education has a hidden informal curriculum which reinforces dominant white culture as being superior; he accuses the educational system in the UK of being ethnocentric. Johal and Bains state that many children wear a 'white mask' in order to fit in to the majority culture. Tony Sewell believes that young black males feel excluded by education as they feel that their teachers who are mainly white are racist as they label all black boys as being deviant and believe that they have no interest in education. Sewell believes this is why many young black males exaggerate their masculinity and that they hold popular culture icons such as P Diddy and 50 cent in high status, as these black role models represent that for black males success will only be possible outside of education. Wright found that the black girls in her study felt that teachers had different expectations of them and treated them unfairly.

Family is another agent of socialisation that reinforces ethnic identity. It could be argued as more important than education as your family is the one to teach you your ethnic norms and values. Francis and Archer's study of Chinese families found that the family played an important role in Chinese children's success in education; this was because Chinese families valued education and this value was passed on to their children. Dench's study of Bangladeshi families living in Tower Hamlets found that, for Bangladeshi families, valuing the extended family was very important; this helped to reinforce their ethnic identity.

Now try your own

Now try to write an answer to the question below. Remember to use the guidance above. Ask your teacher to check your answer if you wish.

(c) Outline and briefly evaluate the view that religion is no longer important in creating and reinforcing ethnic identity. (24 marks)

ExamCafé

Age identities

Part (a) questions

This part of the question assesses your knowledge and understanding (AO1) of a concept. In order to write a good answer you will need to:

- write a clear definition of what the concept means
- demonstrate that you understand the question through giving examples.

Examples can be taken from the pre release material or elsewhere. You should spend approximately 5 minutes on this part of the question. It is worth 8 AO1 marks.

Good example

The following answer is a very strong one and covers all the points mentioned above. Read the answer and highlight where the candidate has given the definition and examples which illustrate it.

(a) Define the concept of 'age'. (8 marks)

Student answer

Age is one of the forms of categorisation that we have in our society. One way of defining age can be to consider it chronologically. As people get older they take on different roles and their social status increases, for example once you become an adult society views you as more responsible. This is evident in the fact that you have to be 18 to be able to drink alcohol in licensed premises. Age can also be defined by life stages; people pass through the three main life stages of youth, middle age and old age, and at each stage individuals adopt different roles and status. For example when you are young you adopt the role of being cared for as the son or daughter of your parents; by the time you are middle aged you take on the role of being the carer for your own children and your status is increased as you are now in a more responsible role.

Example to improve

The example below could be improved. Using the guidance above try to identify what this answer does not do. Then rewrite the answer trying to cover all the points in the checklist.

(a) Define the concept of 'old age'. (8 marks)

Student answer

Old age is a social construction as one person's idea of old age may differ from another's. Old age is the final state of the life course; it is a time when people have come to the end of their career and will have to retire. Some factors associated with old age are loneliness, having poor health and being dependent on others. Old people on television are generally represented in vulnerable positions i.e. living in care homes, in which they take on the role of someone being cared for and they have a lower status than their carers.

Now try your own

Now try to write an answer to the question below. Remember to use the guidance above. Ask your teacher to check your answer if you wish.

(a) Define the concept of 'middle age'. (8 marks)

Part (b) questions

This part of the question assesses your knowledge and understanding (AO1) and your interpretation and application (AO2a) of sociological ideas. It is worth 16 marks: 12 marks for AO1 and 4 marks for AO2a. You should:

- refer to concepts, research studies, examples and, if relevant, theory
- write two clear paragraphs – one for each point and should refer to at least one piece of sociological research in each.

You should spend approximately 15 minutes on part (b).

Good example

The following answer is a very strong one and covers all the points mentioned above. Read the answer and highlight where the candidate has referred to a concept, research study or example.

(b) Outline and explain two ways in which secondary socialisation reinforces age identity. (16 marks)

Student answer

Age identity is reinforced by the secondary agents of socialisation; one of the most important agents in this process is the mass media. The media represents the life stages of youth, middle age and old age in different ways. Muncie (2004) argued that young people are often represented in a negative way; Muncie states that youths are over-represented as deviant and troublesome. This is evident in a lot of the tabloid coverage of young people; the media has created moral panics about young people and gang life. Stan Cohen, in his research on the 'mods and rockers', found that the media had exaggerated the conflict between the two youth groups and had unnecessarily panicked the general public. Muncie also states that the media represent middle age as a time of crisis and old age as a time of dependency and loneliness. However, there have been some recent positive representations of old age in the media. In 2007 the BBC documentary called 'Power to the people; The Great Granny chart invasion' launched the pop group 'The Zimmers'. This pop group was made up of over 60s; they had chart success with the song 'My Generation' and 'Firestarter', a song that was originally performed by the dance group 'The Prodigy'.

Age identity is also reinforced by the workplace; entering into work is marked by the turning of a certain age, and the Children and Young Persons Act of 1933 was amended in 1998 and allowed children to work part time from the age of 14, although they are limited to working five hours on a Saturday and only 2 hours on a Sunday. When you turn 16 years you are legally allowed to work full time; this marks an important part of your 'life-course'. Your age will also determine how much you will be paid, as the minimum wage differs depending on your age; if you are under 18 years old you have a lower financial status than someone who is 25 years old. Turning 'old' is generally marked by the official retirement age of 65 years old. However, not everyone stops work at the retirement age, many famous actors and actresses such as Jack Nicholson and Helen Mirren are still working way past the retirement age of 65 years old.

Example to improve

The example below could be improved. Using the guidance above try to identify what this answer does not do. Then rewrite the answer trying to cover all the points in the checklist.

(b) Outline and explain two ways in which the agents of socialisation reinforce middle age. (16 marks)

Student answer

One agent that reinforces middle age identity is the family. By the time a person reaches middle age their immediate family may have grown up and moved away. This can make the middle aged person feel lost and that they no longer have a distinct role; they also feel that their status is lower. Their role within the family may change; they may go from being a mother or father to being a grandparent, and this role generally carries a lower status than being a parent. Children within the family will reinforce their parents' age by seeing them as middle aged, they view them in this way based on their role and status as parents. Parents are the first to enforce informal social control on their children, so their children are always going to view them as being older, as children associate power and status with control as from an early age within the family we are told to respect our elders, such as parents and grandparents.

Another agent that reinforces middle age is the workplace as many middle aged people are overlooked at work and experience work discrimination. This could be due to employers viewing them as nearing the end of their life course and therefore they may not want to invest training and money in middle aged employees who would be entitled to retire in 10 or 20 years' time. Many middle aged people have experienced age discrimination in the workplace; due to employers viewing them as having less status than their younger counterparts. This may lead to them not being promoted or getting new jobs as they may be considered 'too old'.

Now try your own

Now try to write an answer to the question below. Remember to use the guidance above. Ask your teacher to check your answer if you wish.

(b) Outline and explain two ways in which the agents of socialisation reinforce the period of youth. (16 marks)

Part (c) questions

This part of the question assesses your knowledge and understanding (AO1), your interpretation and application skills (AO2a) and your analysis and evaluation skills (AO2b). It is worth 24 marks: 12 marks for AO1, 8 marks for AO2a, and 4 marks for AO2b. You should:

- refer to concepts, research studies, examples and, if relevant, theory
- make some evaluative points.

You should spend approximately 20 minutes on part (c).

Good example

The following answer is a very strong one and covers all the points mentioned above. Read the answer and highlight where the candidate has referred to a concept, research study, example or made an evaluative point.

(c) Outline and briefly evaluate the view that middle age is a meaningless concept. (24 Marks)

Student answer

This essay will consider the view that middle age is a meaningless concept. The term middle age is used alongside the two other main life stages: youth and old age. Victor (2005) describes the middle years as a distinct phase of life related to people in their forties and fifties before the onset of old age. During our life span the middle years are considered as a time of changing norms and values: the holiday destinations that people go to in their youth, such as the 18-30 holiday packages, no longer seem suitable and middle aged people may opt for a more relaxing holiday than an active one. Middle age is also seen as a period of upheaval where the roles of parent and carer become redundant as children leave home. Due to this the middle years can be seen as a time of lower status for an individual, as many middle aged people have experienced age discrimination in the workplace and are told that they are 'too old' for a particular job role (Waugh et al, 2008). However Bradley (1996) argues that in many other ways middle age can bring with it a higher status for people, much higher than the status of young or old people.

It has been argued by sociologists that the use of the term 'middle age' as a defining stage in the life-course is misleading, as it is argued that middle age is experienced so diversely by people it is meaningless to try and define it. Middle age is stereotypically portrayed differently for men and women. For women, middle age is seen as a time of drastic change, in particular the menopause, and for men it is seen as a time of crisis; men will try to rekindle their youth by buying fast cars and going to the gym. However, consumer culture does clearly identify the middle years as a distinct part of the life-course. Andrew Blaikie (1999) stated that sociologists have become more interested in the middle aged as the consumer industries have taken a greater interest in this group, as they have become an important market for goods and services. The consumer industries have produced middle aged grooming products such as L'Oreal age defying serums for both men and women.

Another reason for the view that the use of the term 'middle age' is meaningless is that there is no official or legal age boundary to help locate where middle age starts or finishes. Generally it is considered as an attitude of mind, characterised by the way middle aged people view life. However, there are social markers that could determine the onset of middle age; for example, the family is very important in reinforcing middle age – as parents enter their middle years they start a new phase where they become the grand parents and they lose their status as the authority figure over their own children, as their children are grown and are fully independent of their parents.

In conclusion it is not clear where middle age begins or ends, however there does appear to be socially constructed markers which indicate where the middle aged part of the life-course takes part.

Example to improve

The example below could be improved. Using the guidance above try to identify what this answer does not do. Then rewrite the answer trying to cover all the points in the checklist.

(c) Outline and briefly evaluate the view that the media is responsible for creating and reinforcing age identity. (24 marks)

Student answer

The media is responsible for creating and reinforcing age identity because it represents age in very distinct categories. Young people are represented as deviant and as victims; this is evident in the newspaper coverage of young people and knife crime (Muncie, 2004). Many moral panics have been created about young people; this is not a new thing as the media has always placed young people in the role of being deviant. Stan Cohen in his studying of the 'mods and rockers' found that the media exaggerated the behaviour of the youth group, they only printed stories and used headlines which represented young people in the roles of criminal and deviant. Sarah Thornton also found in her study of dance culture and young people that the media was instrumental in creating youth culture and reinforcing the period of youth as being one of rebellion and risk taking. Middle aged people are represented as a distinct group who constantly want to be young again; there are a number of grooming products from anti-age creams to hair dyes for men and women in order to fight the signs of ageing and recapture lost youth; this is evident in the L'Oreal adverts. The media represent the period of middle age as one in which this is your time for success and a period where you have a higher status than you do when you are young. This is evident in the representation of the middle aged on television; many of the middle aged people on TV take on the role of being the expert; they are shown to be successful and something that young people should aspire to; examples of this are Alan Sugar in 'The Apprentice' and the business men and women in 'Dragons' Den'. Both of these are on BBC 1 and both of these programmes represent the middle years as a time of being powerful and successful. Old people are represented in a limited way; they are represented as victims, with young people being the perpetrators of criminal acts against old people. Old people in the media are represented as having a lower status than the middle aged or young people. On television old people generally play roles such as the 'grandparent'. The roles represented are very limited and stereotypical.

Now try your own

Now try to write an answer to the question below. Remember to use the guidance above. Ask your teacher to check your answer if you wish.

(c) Outline and briefly evaluate the view that the workplace is responsible for creating and reinforcing old age. (24 marks)

ExamCafé

Pre-release questions

'A View from the Girls'

Burman, M (2004)

Adapted from *Sociology Review*, April 2004

'A View from the Girls' is a study on girls' and young women's thoughts and opinions in relation to violence. The research was an attempt to understand whether girls and young women were actually becoming more violent. Media representations have given the impression that girls are becoming more violent and the aim of Burman's research was to find out if this was actually the case.

The research study used a mixed methods approach which incorporated self report questionnaires, focus group interviews, individual in-depth interviews and a collection of field notes generated from time spent 'hanging about' with the girls. Altogether almost 800 girls participated in the study.

The study was not designed to be representative. It aimed to include a cross section of girls drawn from different backgrounds in order to tap into a wide range of experiences (e.g. girls from different socio-economic, class, cultural and ethnic backgrounds; girls in mainstream education; girls living in care; girls with disabilities).

The research was undertaken in Scotland, in inner city, small town and rural areas. Girls were accessed through schools, secure/residential accommodation, leisure clubs, community groups, voluntary organisations, youth groups and drop-in centres, via outreach workers on the street and through snowball sampling.

Six hundred and seventy girls completed self report questionnaires which asked about the different forms of violence in which they had been involved. Twelve girls took part in in-depth, life history style interviews. Eighteen focus groups were conducted which comprised mostly groups of friends, although some were from the same youth club or school. Using focus groups allowed an insight into the expression of a range of views and experiences of violence and provided a rich source of information. These discussions needed to be managed carefully as the topic was evocative and emotive. Ethical issues were therefore important and there were some challenging moments when disagreements and occasionally even fights broke out.

Burman found that violence by girls was rare. Less than 5% of the girls in the study reported being routinely physically violent, and in focus groups only a small number of girls admitted to using violence against other young people. The majority of girls indicated their use of a range of coping strategies both to manage their own feelings of aggression and to defuse potentially violent encounters with other young people such as talking things out or walking away. Most girls reported acting in a way to avoid the occurrence of violence.

The research also found that girls were less likely to be on the receiving end of violence as they were to witness it. 70% of girls reported witnessing more than 5 incidents in the previous year. Nearly two thirds knew someone, usually another young person, who had been hurt or injured by physical violence. In the main, observing such everyday violence was viewed as 'routine' and 'unremarkable', rather than unusual, which suggests that it is normalised within the context of social interaction experienced by young people.

In all, the findings of the research challenge media depictions of marauding gangs of girls preying on innocent victims and offer a critical alternative to the view that girls are becoming increasingly violent.

Part (d) questions

This part of the exam question assesses your understanding of methodological issues in relation to the pre released material. It is worth 52 marks and you should spend between 45 and 50 minutes answering it. It is worth 20 knowledge and understanding marks (AO1), 12 interpretation and application marks (AO2a) and 20 analysis and evaluation marks (AO2b). You should relate what you write about research methods to the research context in the pre released material and stay focussed on what the question asks you. Planning and structuring your answer will help ensure that you do this. The checklist below will help you ensure that you cover the points that the examiner is looking for.

	Points covered ☑
Have I linked my answer to the context/topic of the research?	
Have I considered the aim of the research in relation to the methods used?	
Have I referred to the key concepts of validity and reliability? (And representativeness and generalisability where relevant?)	
Have I discussed whether the research takes a positivist or interpretivist approach?	
Have I considered both the strengths and weaknesses of the research?	
Have I thoroughly explained each point that I have made?	
Have I carefully addressed the actual question asked?	

Good example

The following answer is a strong one and covers all the points mentioned above. Read the answer and highlight where the candidate has covered each of the points in the checklist below.

Use the checklist above when practising these questions to ensure you gain maximum marks.

(d) Using the pre release material and your own sociological knowledge, explain and evaluate the usefulness of using quantitative and qualitative methods to research girls and violence. (52 marks)

Student answer

The use of both quantitative and qualitative research methods to research girls and violence is very useful. Burman aimed to find out if girls and young women were becoming more violent like the media was suggesting. She used both the quantitative method of self report questionnaires and the qualitative methods of in-depth interviews, focus groups and observations. This meant that she gained a large amount of data and was able to cross-check the different types of data against each other to improve accuracy and ensure validity and reliability. She therefore used triangulation in this piece of research.

Using the quantitative method of self report questionnaires ensured that a large amount of quantitative data was collected as 670 questionnaires were administered. This gave the study an element of reliability as statistical data was generated because the questionnaires consisted of closed questions, and due to the large sample it is likely that if the research was to be repeated, similar results would be found. Using quantitative methods reflects a positivist approach to carrying out research. Positivist sociologists believe that research should be carried out in a scientific way with as much control as possible to ensure reliability. The self report aspect of the questionnaires could also give greater validity to the research as the respondents would not be influenced by the researcher when giving their answers. However, this could also lead to reduced validity as the respondents may not have understood the questions correctly, there may not have been options available which reflected the answer they wished to give and there is little opportunity for them to explain their answers. The girls could also have discussed their responses with their friends and may not have been totally honest. The fact that the topic was about a sensitive and also criminal matter may have meant that the girls lied when giving their responses. Nevertheless, as self report questionnaires are confidential, this would have increased the likelihood of them telling the truth, and therefore increased the validity of the findings.

The other methods used in the study ensured that a large amount of qualitative data was gathered. Qualitative research methods are favoured by interpretivist sociologists. Interpretivists believe that research methods should aim to gather an in-depth understanding of topics covered from the perspective of the respondent themselves. In this study, the use of in-depth interviews and focus groups meant that the girls were able to explain their answers fully from their own perspective and give detailed information and this gave the study greater validity. They would have been able to ask for clarification if needed and the researcher would have been able to probe the respondents for further information. This meant that the researchers were able to gain a better understanding of girls' experiences of violence and the reasons why it may occur. However, such methods did raise some ethical issues as some of the respondents became upset or angry when the topic was raised. Carrying out focus group interviews meant that respondents may have felt more comfortable with their peers and therefore they may have been more open thus increasing validity. However, some respondents may have dominated the discussion and others may have been shy which could have reduced the validity of the study as well as decreasing the representativeness. Also, with a topic such as violence some girls may have exaggerated in order to appear stronger and some may have covered up the fact they were victims of crime in order not to appear vulnerable. This would reduce the validity of the findings.

It is evident that using a mixed method approach to studying girls and violence is very useful. By collecting both quantitative and qualitative data the researchers could add meaning to the statistics that were generated by the questionnaires. Yet, by gaining statistical data as well, a degree of precision and reliability was added. Combining the methods can mean that the strengths of some overcame the weaknesses of others ensuring that the findings are both reliable and valid. However, the mixed methods approach is very time consuming and can generate a large amount of data which can be difficult to analyse. Problems may occur if the different methods used throw up different findings. However, in relation to the topic of girls and violence it is very useful as conclusions can be drawn as to whether girls were becoming more violent through the statistical data and these conclusions can be understood through the gathering of qualitative data.

'Comparing Co-education and Single Sex Schooling'

O'Leary (2002)

Adapted from *Sociology Review*, November, 2002

'Comparing co-education and single sex schooling' is a study into co-education and whether it has a negative impact on the educational attainment of girls. The study aimed to find out whether co-education resulted in poorer exam performance for girls, whether it affected students' personal and social development and what accounts for any differences between co-educational and single sex schools in exam performance and student development.

The study was one of the largest studies of co-education in the world and took a quantitative approach. 116 secondary level schools were visited and over ten thousand students completed questionnaires. School principals and career guidance counsellors were interviewed. The schools were a stratified random sample of the different types of school in the Irish education system. Secondary, vocational and comprehensive schools were all included.

The researchers obtained official lists of the students and the classes in the schools and they decided on the students to ensure that they had a representative sample of students in each school. The questionnaire which was completed by students included questions about their social backgrounds, various dimensions of their schooling, their career aspirations and academic expectations. These are factors which are identified in the international literature on schooling as being relevant to student experience and performance. Students were asked which subjects they were studying and why they had chosen those subjects. This was to investigate whether schools had channelled students by gender into particular subjects and whether the practice varied in other types of schools.

The researchers attempted to measure student experiences, such as those of teacher-student interaction, through questionnaire scales, which included items such as 'How often have you been praised by a teacher?' to examine whether teacher-student interaction was different in co-educational and single sex schools. They also obtained students' exam results and compared them with their prior expectations. Details of ability tests taken by the students before they entered the school were also obtained to enable us to examine how the students had performed in the school compared to their ability on entry.

The study was not only concerned with academic performance and career aspirations, but also considered personal and social development. For example, the questionnaire asked about self confidence. It also inquired about their perception of their own appearance. Advanced statistical techniques were employed to give an accurate estimate of the effects of co-education, over and above other student and school factors.

The research found that co-educational and single sex schools differed in a number of ways. Single sex schools tended to be more selective in their intake and took students who were academically brighter and from higher social classes. They also found that girls at single sex schools do slightly better in terms of average exam grades than girls in co-educational schools. The effect of co-education was found to be greatest among lower ability students. Co-education was found to have a clear negative effect on girls' performance in mathematics.

However, the researchers concluded that the negative effects of co-education are relatively small and mainly confined to a few specific aspects of school experience. Other factors such as family background and individual ability as well as school effectiveness continue to matter most, even if they are not as visible as the gender composition of the school.

Example to improve: 'Comparing Co-education and Single Sex Schooling'

The example below could be improved. Using the guidance in the checklist above try to identify what this answer does not do. Then rewrite the answer trying to cover all the points in the checklist.

(d) Using the pre release material and your own sociological knowledge explain and evaluate the use of quantitative methods to research whether there is any difference in the effects of co-educational and single sex schooling. (52 marks)

Student answer

Quantitative methods are appropriate to study the difference in the effects of co-education and single sex schooling as they enable research to gather statistical data and therefore measure the difference. Using quantitative methods such as questionnaires also means that the researchers can target a large sample and gain more representative findings.

Using closed questions in the questionnaire means that the respondents have limited choice over what to say and it is likely that if the study was repeated similar findings would be found.

However, using the questionnaire method may mean that data gathered is not accurate. Respondents may misinterpret questions or may wish to give an answer which is not available to them. They may lie in front of their friends. School age respondents may be more likely to give socially desirable answers as they are at an age when peer pressure is an influence.

Sociology of the family

Revision checklist

The list below outlines all the topics and sub topics which you need to cover in your revision. Your teacher/s may have taught you other sociological research studies in which case you should also revise these. The studies referred to below can all be found in the core text book.

Key concepts and key trends within the family

Key concepts:

- Nuclear families ☐
- Extended families ☐
- Households ☐

Trends (including statistics where relevant) over the past 30 years:

- Family size ☐
- Marriage ☐
- Divorce ☐
- Cohabitation ☐
- Single parent families ☐
- Single person households ☐

The role of the family within society

- Functionalist theories (Murdoch, Parsons) ☐
- Evaluation of functionalist theories ☐
- Marxist theories (Engels, Zaretsky) ☐
- Evaluation of Marxist theories ☐

Family diversity

- Single parent families ☐
- Beanpole families ☐
- Reconstituted families ☐
- Cultural diversity ☐
- Class diversity ☐
- Sexual diversity ☐
- New right views on diversity and evaluation ☐
- New Labour views on diversity and evaluation ☐
- Postmodernist views on diversity and evaluation ☐

Roles, responsibilities and relationships between…

Men and women

- Giddens ☐
- Willmott and Young ☐
- Anne Oakley ☐
- Duncombe and Marsden ☐
- Warner ☐
- Garrod ☐
- Edgell ☐
- Pahl ☐
- Dobash and Dobash ☐

Children and parents

- Gatrell ☐
- Hatter ☐
- Garrod ☐
- Duncan ☐

Explanations and evaluation

- Functionalist explanations (Parsons) and evaluation ☐
- Marxist explanations (Zaretsky) and evaluation ☐
- Feminist explanations (Liberal, Marxist, Radical) and evaluation ☐
- Demographic changes (ageing population and family size) ☐

Key concepts 

This recap activity will ensure that you go over those all-important key concepts. Complete the key concept chart by writing a definition of the concept and, where possible, include which sociologist uses it. Refer to your core text book or your classroom notes.

Key concepts	Definitions
Nuclear family	
Extended family	
Families of choice	
Voluntary childlessness	
Instrumental needs	
Expressive needs	
Warm bath theory	
Sexual division of labour	
Reconstituted family	
Beanpole family	
Conjugal roles	
Confluent love	
Triple shift	
Familial ideology	

Mix and match

The purpose of this exercise is to get you to test your knowledge on key pieces of sociological research within the topic of the family. You will need to match the explanation of the research/theory with the title of the study. Each sociologist/title of study is numbered and the explanation of the study is lettered. Match the correct research with the title of the study by drawing a connecting line from one to the other. Then check at the bottom of the page to see if you have matched the two correctly.

1 'Cereal packet family'

2 The Divorce Reform Act of 1969

3 Murdoch (1949)

4 Functionalist

5 Zaretsky (1976)

6 Allan and Crow (2001)

7 'Sandwich generation'

8 Warner (2005)

9 A Thompson et al (2005)

A
Grundy and Henretta (2006) use a concept to try to explain the position of women between the ages of 55 and 69, who cater for the needs of both their needy parents and their own children.

B
This researcher found that most home-based mothers today worked around 100 hours per week

C
In 1967 Leach argued that the media represented the family in a certain way. This family image included the male breadwinner/female housewife with two kids.

D
These sociologists' study into fathers found that 80% of them would be happy to be 'stay at home' fathers.

E
This change to government legislation allowed couples to separate on the grounds of 'irretrievable breakdown'.

F
This Marxist supporter argues that housewives are important in promoting capitalist ideology, by performing free household tasks in the home and socialising children to be compliant workers of the future.

G
This theoretical view believes that the nuclear family is a better 'fit' and ideal form of family within industrial societies.

H
This sociologist believed that the four functions of the nuclear family were: economic, educational, sexual and reproductive.

I
These sociologists challenge the assumptions made about single parents. They argue that they do not have differing norms and values from the nuclear family. Furthermore, at some point single parents do form a two-parent structure.

Answers: 1.C, 2.E, 3.H, 4.G, 5.F, 6.I, 7.A, 8.B, 9.D

Check your knowledge quick fire quiz

This multiple choice quiz will test your knowledge on the four areas of the family: key concepts, the role of the family, family diversity and roles and responsibilities. Each question is worth a number of points; the points are indicated at the end of the question. The more points a question is worth, the more difficult it is. Top mark questions reflect whether you have read your core text book thoroughly. Once you have ticked the answer you believe to be correct, add up your score to reveal whether you are a sociology of the family expert!

1 *Whose research found that children from co-parenting families were often enthusiastic about having 'two of everything'?* **(2 points)**

a) ☐ Parsons (1960s)
b) ☐ Smart (2000)
c) ☐ Oakley (1982)

2 *In Berthoud and Beishon's (1997) analysis of the fourth National Survey of Ethnic Minorities PSI data, which ethnic group did they identify as having the highest rate of divorce and separation?* **(3 points)**

a) ☐ White Irish
b) ☐ British South Asians
c) ☐ British African-Caribbean

3 *Whose study into the role of the Chinese family and their children's educational achievement found that Chinese families used their skills, networks and money to further their children's educational achievement?* **(2 points)**

a) ☐ Singh (2003)
b) ☐ Modood (1997)
c) ☐ Archer and Francis (2006)

4 *What is the process called that was identified by Bourdieu, which explains the upper class child's advantage of being socialised into high culture by their parents?* **(4 points)**

a) ☐ Social capital
b) ☐ Cultural capital
c) ☐ Human capital

5 *Whose research into family diversity found that there was a growing focus on friendship; friends were adopting the roles normally undertaken by family members?* **(3 points)**

a) ☐ Allan and Crow (2001)
b) ☐ Roseneil and Budgeon (2004)
c) ☐ Talcott Parsons (1967)

6 *Which theoretical view sees the increase of divorce and the rise of cohabitation as a sign of 'moral decline' in contemporary society?* **(3 points)**

a) ☐ Functionalist
b) ☐ New right
c) ☐ Interactionist

7 *Which theoretical view 'deconstructs' the existing ideas of 'traditional' family life and promotes the idea of 'choice'?* **(3 points)**

a) ☐ Feminist
b) ☐ Postmodern
c) ☐ Functionalist

8 *Whose research into young mothers found that there were positive effects of motherhood, such as an increase in self-esteem and feelings of security and stability?* **(2 points)**

a) ☐ Somervielle (2002)
b) ☐ Thompson et al (2005)
c) ☐ Bell et al (2004)

9 *Which feminists argue that the family as a unit is patriarchal and promotes sexism through the 'taken for granted' assumption that the 'triple shift' is the norm for women?* **(3 points)**

a) ☐ Radical feminist
b) ☐ Liberal feminist
c) ☐ Marxist feminist

Possible 25 points

19–25 Well done! You are definitely a sociology of the family expert!
12–18 It's official: you are becoming a 'sociology star'!
7–11 Looks like you might be avoiding the more difficult questions – get back to reading that text book!
0–6 Oh dear: you're not going to win any 'sociology student of the year' prizes!

Answers: 1.b, 2.c, 3.c, 4.b, 5.b, 6.b, 7.b, 8.c, 9.a

Theory identifier

The statements below reflect the viewpoints of one of the following theories – functionalism, Marxism, radical feminism, Marxist feminism, liberal feminism, new right, new Labour or postmodernism. Identify which theory goes with which statement by writing in the space above the statement.

1 ____________________

The family helps ensure that members are healthy and fit so that they can work hard under capitalism and so their labour can be exploited.

2 ____________________

The family has many functions including education, economic, sexual and reproductive.

3 ____________________

Families evolved with the ownership of private property. In order to ensure that property and wealth were passed on to the sons, families had to be monogamous.

4 ____________________

In the UK today there are a diverse range of family types including gay, reconstituted and single person households.

5 ____________________

The family is a dangerous place for women. They are often subjected to violence, abuse and the control of their husbands.

6 ____________________

Women are the slaves of wage slaves. They do hours and hours of domestic work which is unpaid and this is beneficial for capitalism.

7 ____________________

The nuclear family is the ideal family type within industrial societies.

8 ____________________

The nuclear family type is superior to others. Single parent families are dysfunctional and often lead to the children not being effectively socialised.

9 ____________________

Although men may now help more with domestic roles and childcare this still remains the main responsibility of the woman. There should be more policies introduced to enable men to take an equal role in housework and childcare.

10 ____________________

The change in family types and increase in diversity should be acknowledged and social policies should account for this.

Answers: 1. Marxism, 2. functionalism, 3. Marxism, 4. postmodernism, 5. radical feminism, 6. Marxist feminism, 7. functionalism, 8. new right, 9. liberal feminism, 10. new Labour

Applying research studies task

The following is a list of some of the key concepts you may need to refer to when answering questions on the sociology of the family. Fill in the spaces in the adjacent column with details of a sociologist and research study which could be used to illustrate each concept. The first one is done for you. Answers can be found at the back of the book.

Key Concept	Sociologist/Research Study
Single person households	Chandler (2004) found that the number of young people living in single person households had grown, particularly amongst men aged 25–44.
Beanpole families	
Co-parenting	
Same sex families	
Emotion work	
Domestic violence	
Dads	
Ageing population	

Sociology of health

Revision checklist

The list below outlines all the topics and sub topics which you need to cover in your revision. Your teacher/s may have taught you other sociological research studies in which case you should also revise these. The studies referred to below can all be found in the core text book.

Key concepts

- Health ☐
- Illness ☐
- Sickness ☐
- Bio-medical approaches ☐
- Social model of health ☐
- Morbidity and mortality rates ☐

Social construction of health and illness

- Cultural relativity ☐
- The social process of becoming ill ☐
- Lay definitions ☐

Patterns and explanations of ill health in society

- Ill health and social class (statistics) ☐
- Ill health and gender (statistics) ☐
- Ill health and ethnicity (statistics) ☐
- Artefact explanations ☐
- Social selection explanations ☐
- Cultural explanations ☐
- Structural explanations ☐

The social construction of mental illness and disability

- Ethnicity and mental illness (definitions, diagnosis and trends) ☐
- Class and mental illness (definitions, diagnosis and trends) ☐
- Gender and mental illness (definitions, diagnosis and trends) ☐
- Structural explanations ☐
- Evaluation of structural explanations ☐
- Interactionist explanations (Foucault, Goffman) ☐
- Evaluation of interactionist explanations ☐
- Disability (medical and social models) ☐

The role of health professionals in society

- Functionalist theories (Parsons) ☐
- Evaluation of functionalist theories ☐
- Marxist theories (Navarro) ☐
- Evaluation of Marxist theories ☐
- Weberian theories (Friedson) ☐
- Evaluation of Weberian theories ☐
- Feminist theories (Abbot and Wallace) ☐
- Evaluation of feminist theories ☐
- Postmodernist theories (Senior, Foucault, Hunt and Lightly) ☐
- Evaluation of postmodernist theories ☐
- Rise of complementary/alternative medicine ☐

Key concepts

This recap activity will ensure that you go over those all-important key concepts. Complete the key concept chart by writing a definition of the concept and, where possible, include which sociologist uses it. Refer to your core text book or your classroom notes.

Key concepts	Definitions
WHO	
Bio-medical model	
Social model	
Latrogenesis	
Artefact explanations	
Victim blaming	
Learned helplessness	
Disability	
Disablism	
Universalism	
Affective neutrality	
Discourse (Foucault)	
Mortality	
Morbidity	

Mix and match 

The purpose of this exercise is to get you to test your knowledge on key pieces of sociological research within the topic of health. You will need to match the explanation of the research/theory with the title of the study. Each sociologist/ title of study is numbered and the explanation of the study is lettered. Match the correct research with the title of the study by drawing a connecting line from one to the other. Then check at the bottom of the page to see if you have matched the two correctly.

1 Illich (2002)

2 Biomedical model

3 Taylor et al (1996)

4 Shaw and Davey Smith (2005)

5 Cultural

6 Macintyre (1992)

7 Amin (1992)

8 Foucault (1973)

9 Hyde (2001)

A This sociologist found that men were more likely to overrate their symptoms compared with women; this could lead to an underestimation of gender morbidity statistics.

B This sociologist is critical of the way modern medicine defines illness. He argues that we can only function effectively in terms of health if we accept our less than perfect physical and mental condition.

C This sociologist argued that ethnic minorities are concentrated in more hazardous work, therefore are exposed to more accidents and work related illness.

D This approach takes a scientific point of view of health and believes that illness and disease can be treated and cured.

E This sociologist argues that health and illness are relative. A person's idea of health is related to and reflects their theories of disease and health.

F These sociologists measured the relationship between poverty and life expectancy by comparing affluent and poor areas of the UK between the period of 1992 and 2003. Their study found that health inequality is increasing.

G This explanation of health inequality can be argued as 'blaming the victim'. This view has been commonplace in government thinking and policy.

H This sociologist believes that people with impairments are excluded by a social environment which is inaccessible and discriminatory and which favours the biomedical definition of disability.

I This theorist argues that to use the term 'mental illness' reflects a particular discourse. Furthermore the use of language such as 'symptoms' and 'disease' reflect the power of the medical profession.

Answers: 1.B, 2.D, 3.E, 4.F, 5.G, 6.A, 7.C, 8.I, 9.H

Check your knowledge quick fire quiz:

This multiple choice quiz will test your knowledge on the four areas of health: the key concepts and the social construction of health, patterns and explanations of ill health, the social construction of mental illness and disability, the role of health professionals in society. Each question is worth a number of points; the points are indicated at the end of the question. The more points a question is worth, the more difficult it is. Top mark questions reflect whether you have read your core text book thoroughly. Once you have ticked the answer you believe to be correct, add up your score to reveal whether you have a very 'healthy' understanding of the sociology of health!

1 *When was the Disability Discrimination Act (DDA) passed?* (**2 points)**

a) ☐ 1999
b) ☐ 2001
c) ☐ 1995

2 *Who argued that, once labelled, a mentally ill person goes through three phases: the process of mortification, learning a new social role and responding to the label of 'mentally ill'?* **(2 points)**

a) ☐ Foucault (1973)
b) ☐ Weber (1958)
c) ☐ Goffman (1968)

3 *Which perspective argues that women are prescribed minor drugs and anti-depressants in greater quantities than men? The drugs are used as a form of social control which transforms social problems into medical ones.* **(3 points)**

a) ☐ Interactionist
b) ☐ Marxist
c) ☐ Feminist

4 *Which explanation believes that the causes of mental illness are to be found within society and not in the individual's body?* **(4 points)**

a) ☐ Cultural
b) ☐ Structural
c) ☐ Interactionist

5 *How many times more likely are men to commit suicide compared to women?* **(3 points)**

a) ☐ Three times more likely
b) ☐ Twice as likely
c) ☐ The same

6 *Whose research of the definition of health, carried out on the elderly in Aberdeen, identified the following three lay concepts of health: health as an absence of disease, health as a dimension of strength, weakness, exhaustion and health as functional fitness?* **(3 points)**

a) ☐ Blaxter (1990)
b) ☐ Williams (1983)
c) ☐ Taylor et al (1996)

7 *Which theorist argued that the medical profession gained dominance by creating and controlling a new scientific high status language?* **(3 points)**

a) ☐ McKeown (1976)
b) ☐ Sheeran (1995)
c) ☐ Foucault (1973)

Possible 20 points

17–20 Well done! Your knowledge of sociology is extremely healthy!
12–16 It's official: you are becoming a 'sociology star'!
7–11 Looks like you might be avoiding the more difficult questions – get back to reading that text book!
0–6 Oh dear: you're not going to win any 'sociology student of the year' prizes!

Answers: 1.c, 2.c, 3.c, 4.b, 5.a, 6.b, 7.c

Theory identifier

The statements below reflect the viewpoints of one of the following theories – functionalism, Marxism, Weberianism, feminism or postmodernism. Identify which theory goes with which statement by writing in the space above the statement.

1 ______________________

The medical professions serve to promote the interests of the ruling class through acting in a gatekeeper role and through private medicine.

2 ______________________

No single model of health can be seen as the 'truth'. People now have access to a whole range of models of health and explanations from which they can choose.

3 ______________________

Medicine seeks to control women who deviate from traditional femininity. For example, female contraception carries significant health risks which men would not be prepared to tolerate.

4 ______________________

The real causes of ill health are poverty and material deprivation generated by the capitalist system.

5 ______________________

Sales of alternative medicine have grown and this is becoming increasingly popular in contemporary society.

6 ______________________

The medical professions receive high status and rewards because they perform the vital function of controlling illness and helping vulnerable people.

7 ______________________

The medical professions operate to serve their own interests. They gain high status and rewards through operating social closure and ensuring professional dominance.

8 ______________________

Men make up the majority of senior positions within the medical professions and women are seen to play more of a 'helper' role as nurses and midwives.

Answers: 1. Marxism, 2. postmodernism, 3. feminism, 4. Marxism, 5. postmodernism, 6. functionalism, 7. Weberianism, 8. feminism

Applying research studies task

The following is a list of some of the key concepts you may need to refer to when answering questions on the sociology of health. Fill in the spaces in the adjacent column with details of a sociologist and research study which could be used to illustrate each concept. The first one is done for you. Answers can be found at the back of the book.

Key Concept	Sociologist/Research Study
Social model of health	Nettleton (2006) points out that health and disease are socially patterned. Illness is not randomly distributed, there are clear patterns in relation to gender, class and ethnicity.
Disease	
Health	
Biomedical model of health	
Mental illness	
Disability	
Alternative medicine	
Orthodox medicine	

Sociology of religion

Revision checklist

The list below outlines all the topics and sub topics which you need to cover in your revision. Your teacher/s may have taught you other sociological research studies, in which case you should also revise these. The studies referred to below can all be found in the core text book.

Key concepts and the changing nature of religious movements in society

Key concepts:

- Religious belief ☐
- Religious commitment ☐
- Religious membership ☐
- Religiosity ☐

Different types of religious institution and movements:

- Churches ☐
- Denominations ☐
- New religious movements ☐
- New Age movements ☐
- Religious fundamentalism ☐

The role of religion in society

- Functionalist theories (Durkheim, Malinowski) ☐
- Evaluation of functionalist theories ☐
- Marxist theories (Marx) ☐
- Evaluation of Marxist theories ☐
- Weberian theories (Weber) ☐
- Evaluation of Weberian theories ☐
- Postmodernist theories ☐

Religion and social position

Patterns and trends…

- Religiosity and ethnicity (statistics and explanations) ☐
- Religiosity and gender (statistics and explanations) ☐
- Religiosity and social class (statistics and explanations) ☐
- Religiosity and age (statistics and explanations) ☐
- New religious movements/ New age movements (trends and explanations) ☐

The strength of religion in society

Evidence and explanations that secularisation is taking place:

- Bruce ☐
- Wilson ☐

Evidence and explanations that secularisation is not taking place:

- Stark ☐
- Davie ☐

Key concepts

This recap activity will ensure that you go over those all-important key concepts. Complete the key concept chart by writing a definition of the concept and where possible include which sociologist uses it. Refer to your core text book or your classroom notes.

Key concepts	Definitions
Inclusive definition	
Exclusive definition	
Sects	
Religious pluralism	
New Religious Movements (NRMs)	
New Agers	
Holistic milieu	
Fundamentalism	
Secularisation	
Opium of the people	
Liberation theology	
Salvation anxiety	
Symbolic exclusion	
Disengagement	
Theodicy	
Religiosity	
Calvinism	

Mix and match

The purpose of this exercise is to get you to test your knowledge on key pieces of sociological research within the topic of religion. You will need to match the explanation of the research/theory with the title of the study. Each sociologist/title of study is numbered and the explanation of the study is lettered. Match the correct research with the title of the study by drawing a connecting line from one to the other. Then check at the bottom of the page to see if you have matched the two correctly.

1 Garrod (2006)

2 Sects

3 Durkheim (1912)

4 Marxism

5 Weberian

6 'Spiritual marketplace'

7 Weber (1958)

8 Davie (1994)

9 Tearfund (2007)

A
This theorist maintained that by worshipping a totem (sacred object) people were in fact worshipping their society, as the totem represented those societies' values.

B
This theory is interested in the meanings that people attach to religion. This theory is from the Symbolic Interactionist school of thought.

C
This sociological researcher looked at children's views of religious belief and found that schools are one of the few places where children from different religious backgrounds meet regularly.

D
Postmodern theorists believe that religion has become a product of consumerism; it can be bought and sold, and they believe that religion is part of a 'pick and mix' culture. They use this concept to try to explain the process of buying and selling religion.

E
This form of religious organisation is exclusive; people have to choose to join, although they do have to meet a certain criteria.

F
This theorist explained the appeal of sects to marginalised groups; the sects can offer a sense of inclusion for those that are marginalised, as they can feel excluded from the wider society.

G
This research found a decline in attendance and membership of religious institutions; it found that 29.3 million are unreceptive and closed to attending church.

H
This theory believes that religion benefits the ruling class, as it promotes the idea that inequality is sanctioned by God. Religion acts as a tool of distraction from real societal issues such as poverty.

I
This sociologist found that men and women view God differently; for women God was about love and comfort, whereas men saw God in terms of power and control.

Answers: 1.C, 2.E, 3.A, 4.H, 5.B, 6.D, 7.F, 8.I, 9.G

Check your knowledge quick fire quiz

This multiple choice quiz will test your knowledge on the four areas of religion: the changing nature of religious movements, the role of religion, religion and social position and the strength of religion in society. Each question is worth a number of points; the points are indicated at the end of the question. The more points a question is worth, the more difficult it is. Top mark questions reflect whether you have read your core text book thoroughly. Once you have ticked the answer you believe to be correct, add up your score to reveal whether you should be worshipped for your extensive knowledge of the sociology of religion!

1 *Research by the Office for National Statistics on religious beliefs of young people found that young people were less likely to be religious compared to people over the age of 65 years. What was the percentage of young people who had no religion?* **(3 points)**

a) ☐ 50%
b) ☐ 30%
c) ☐ 23%

2 *Bruce (1996) argued that New Age movements were mostly adopted by which social group?* **(2 points)**

a) ☐ Upper class
b) ☐ Middle class
c) ☐ Working class

3 *Classical sociologists believed that the key feature of modernity would inevitably lead to secularisation. What was the key feature?* **(3 points)**

a) ☐ Growing affluence
b) ☐ Societalisation
c) ☐ Rationalisation

4 *Martin (1996) argued that comparing figures on past and present religiosity was problematic, as the middle classes in Victorian times attended church out of 'respectability' rather than for faith reasons. What did Martin argue the Victorian attendance figures lacked?* **(4 points)**

a) ☐ Validity
b) ☐ Reliability
c) ☐ Generalisability

5 *Who argues that religiosity is not in decline, and that individuals differentiate between religious belief and religious belonging?* **(3 points)**

a) ☐ Stark (1999)
b) ☐ Voas (2005)
c) ☐ Davie (1994)

6 *Bellah (1975) argued that religious qualities exist in rituals such as national support for England during World Cup events. What is the term coined by Bellah that explains this process?* **(3 points)**

a) ☐ 'Civil Partnership'
b) ☐ 'Civil Nationalism'
c) ☐ 'Civil Religion'

7 *Which sociologist argued that black evangelicalism can give black people a sense of independence and offers them hope?* **(3 points)**

a) ☐ Weber (1958)
b) ☐ Akhtar (2005)
c) ☐ Beckford (2000)

Possible 21 points

17–20 Well done! You are definitely worth worshipping!
12–16 It's official: you are becoming a 'sociology star'!
7–11 Looks like you might be avoiding the more difficult questions – get back to reading that text book!
0–6 Oh dear: you're not going to win any 'sociology student of the year' prizes!

Answers: 1.c, 2.b, 3.c, 4.a, 5.c, 6.c, 7.c

Theory identifier

The statements below reflect the viewpoints of one of the following theories – functionalism, Marxism, Weberianism or postmodernism. Identify which theory goes with which statement by writing in the space above the statement.

1 ______________________

Religion reinforces the social solidarity of society.

2 ______________________

Religion has become a 'pick and mix' culture as there are now a range of religions that people can choose from.

3 ______________________

The aim of religion is to help people make sense of the world around them.

4 ______________________

Religion is the 'opium of the people' – it is like a drug providing relief and comfort from the strains and stresses of living in a capitalist society.

5 ______________________

Religious belief can bring about social and economic change. For example, the beliefs of Calvinist Protestants led to the development of capitalism.

6 ______________________

New religions have emerged and due to globalisation people are following religions from other countries and cultures.

7 ______________________

Religion has a crucial function in teaching the norms and values of society.

8 ______________________

Religion acts as an agent of social control to justify inequality and keep the working class in their place.

9 ______________________

Religion has a function when people are going through a stressful time in their lives, for example, suffering bereavement; it helps them deal with upset or inexplicable events.

Answers: 1. functionalism, 2. postmodernism, 3. Weberianism, 4. Marxism, 5. Weberianism, 6. postmodernism, 7. functionalism, 8. Marxism, 9. functionalism

Applying research studies task

The following is a list of some of the key concepts you may need to refer to when answering questions on the sociology of religion. Fill in the spaces in the adjacent column with details of a sociologist and research study which could be used to illustrate each concept. The first one is done for you. Answers can be found at the back of the book.

Key Concept	Sociologist/Research Study
Civil religion	Bellah (1975) used the term 'civil religion' to refer to the way people are brought together in secular societies through national events and rituals.
Symbolic exclusion	
New Age movements	
Secularisation	
Religious pluralism	
Spirituality	
Religion – inclusive definition	
Religion – exclusive definition	

Sociology of youth

Revision checklist

The list below outlines all the topics and sub topics which you need to cover in your revision. Your teacher/s may have taught you other sociological research studies, in which case you should also use these. The studies referred to below can all be found in the core text book.

Key concepts

- Youth ☐
- Youth culture ☐
- Youth subcultures ☐
- Peer group ☐
- Spectacular subcultures ☐

Social construction of youth

Reasons for the development of youth culture and subcultures:

- Schooling ☐
- Media ☐
- Economy ☐
- Globalisation ☐
- Consumption ☐
- Demographic trends ☐

The role of youth culture/subcultures in society

- Functionalist theories (Parsons, Eisenstadt) ☐
- Marxist theories (CCCS, Hall and Jefferson, Clarke, Hebdidge, Brake) ☐
- Feminist theories (McRobbie and Garber, Smart, Lincoln) ☐
- Postmodernist theories (Thornton, Polemus, Bennett) ☐
- Gender and subcultures (McRobbie and Garber, Smart, Lincoln) ☐
- Ethnicity and subcultures (Rastafarians, Bhangra, Resistance, Hybrid Subcultures, Ethnocentrism) ☐

Youth and Deviance

Key terms:

- Delinquency ☐
- Deviance ☐
- Crime ☐
- Labelling ☐
- Moral panic ☐

Patterns and trends:

- Youth deviance and gender (statistics and explanations) ☐
- Youth deviance and ethnicity (statistics and explanations) ☐
- Youth deviance and class (statistics and explanations) ☐
- Evaluation of functionalist explanations (Albert Cohen) ☐
- Evaluation of Marxist explanations (CCCS) ☐
- Evaluation of the labelling theory (Becker, Stan Cohen) ☐

The Experience of Youth in Education

Social class

- Achievement ☐
- Socialisation ☐
- Experiences in the school ☐

Gender

- Achievement ☐
- Socialisation ☐
- Experiences in the school ☐
- Patterns and trends in subject choices (statistics and explanations) ☐

Ethnicity

- Achievement ☐
- Socialisation ☐
- Experiences in the school ☐

Pro- and anti-school/education subcultures

- Shain ☐
- Archer and Yamashati ☐
- Jackson ☐
- Sewell ☐

Key concepts

This recap activity will ensure that you go over those all-important key concepts. Complete the key concept chart by writing a definition of the concept and, where possible, include which sociologist uses it. Refer to your core text book or your classroom notes.

Key concepts	Definitions
Neo-tribes	
Magical solution	
Incorporation	
Subcultural capital	
Moral panic	
Master status	
Male stream	
Resistance	
Crisis of masculinity	
Ladette	

Mix and match

The purpose of this exercise is to get you to test your knowledge on key pieces of sociological research within the topic of youth. You will need to match the explanation of the research/theory with the title of the study. Each sociologist/title of study is numbered and the explanation of study is lettered. Match the correct research with the title of the study by drawing a connecting line from one to the other. Then check at the bottom of the page to see if you have matched the two correctly.

1
Spectacular youth subcultures

2
Resistance

3
Messerschmidt (1993)

4
Functionalist explanation

5
'Just like a girl' Sue Sharpe (1994)

6
T Sewell (2000)

A
This sociologist argues that it is difficult to obtain data on crime and social class due to the problem of operationalising social class. He states that social class and ethnicity will affect the type of crime that a young person will be drawn to.

B
The CCCS neo-Marxist studies of youth subcultures during the 1950s and 60s identified the groups that emerged as being actively resistant through their flamboyant dress and anti-conforming attitudes.

C
Hall and Jefferson (1976) argued that youth subcultures were reacting against the 'crisis of … capitalism'. By forming alternative subcultural styles young people could undermine hegemonic culture.

D
Comparative study first undertaken in 1972 and then repeated in 1991. This sociologist was interested in female working class experience of compulsory education. Her first study found that the girls valued homemaking; however, in the second, they were much more career orientated.

E
This sociologist found two clear anti-school subcultural groups of resistance within the behaviour of some Afro-Caribbean males. These two groups he identified as the Retreatist and the Rebels.

F
Deviance can be explained as something that young people go through during the transitional period of childhood to adulthood.

Answers: 1.B, 2.C, 3.A, 4.F, 5.D, 6.E

Check your knowledge quick fire quiz

This multiple choice quiz will test your knowledge on the three main areas of youth: subcultures, deviance and schooling. Each question is worth a number of points; the points are indicated at the end of the question. The more points a question is worth, the more difficult it is. Top mark questions reflect whether you have read your core text book thoroughly. Once you have ticked the answer you believe to be correct, add up your score to reveal whether you are a 'spectacular' youth genius!

Youth subcultures

1 *Which of the following sociologists use the idea of 'labelling' to explain how society labels those that have differing norms and values from the majority of society?* **(2 points)**

a) ☐ Tony Sewell
b) ☐ Paul Willis
c) ☐ Howard S. Becker

2 *What does the acronym CCCS stand for?* **(2 points)**

a) ☐ Contemporary Centre for Central Studies
b) ☐ Centre for Citizen Cultural Studies
c) ☐ Centre for Contemporary Cultural Studies

3 *Which feminist sociologist identified a strong 'teeny bopper' subculture, which became known as the 'bedroom culture'?* **(3 points)**

a) ☐ Angela McRobbie
b) ☐ Sarah Thornton
c) ☐ Sue Sharpe

Youth and deviance

4 *Claire Alexander (2000) conducted a study on Asian gangs. What did she argue the media had created in their representation of these gangs?* **(4 points)**

a) ☐ a moral panic
b) ☐ a 'myth of the Asian gang'
c) ☐ amplification of Asian gangs

5 *What is the term used to describe how males are more likely to engage in 'risk-taking behaviour'?* **(3 points)**

a) ☐ hypermasculinity
b) ☐ master status
c) ☐ edgework

Youth in education

6 *Who conducted the research on working class males' experience of education, titled 'Learning to Labour: why working class kids get working class jobs?'* **(3 points)**

a) ☐ Andy Bennett
b) ☐ Paul Hodkinson
c) ☐ Paul Willis

7 *Which piece of legislation ensured that, regardless of gender, ethnicity or social class, all students up to GCSE level were offered the same compulsory subjects?* **(3 points)**

a) ☐ The Education Act of 1944
b) ☐ The Education Reform Act 1988
c) ☐ Curriculum 2000

Possible 20 points

17–20 Well done! You are a spectacular youth genius!
12–16 It's official: you are becoming a 'sociology star'!
7–11 Looks like you might be avoiding the more difficult questions – get back to reading that text book!
0–6 Oh dear: you're not going to win any 'sociology student of the year' prizes!

Answers: 1.c, 2.c, 3.a, 4.b, 5.c, 6.c, 7.b

Theory identifier

The statements below reflect the viewpoints of one of the following theories – functionalism, Marxism, feminism or postmodernism. Identify which theory goes with which statement by writing in the space above the statement.

1 ______________________________
Youth subcultures were formed as a form of resistance to capitalism.

2 ______________________________
Youth subcultures have a function as they help young people manage the transition from childhood to adulthood.

3 ______________________________
Youth subcultures were a magical solution to the problems faced by working class youths.

4 ______________________________
Researchers studying youth subcultures have produced a male stream sociology which has ignored the experiences of female youths.

5 ______________________________
Young people are now able to choose from a supermarket of style options in terms of fashions, music and identities.

6 ______________________________
Young working class people may commit crime as a way of rebelling against the norms and values of capitalist society.

7 ______________________________
Girls have more restrictions placed on their behaviour than boys and as a result form a 'bedroom culture'.

8 ______________________________
The term 'neo tribe' is more useful than 'subculture' and reflects the looser associations that young people now form.

9 ______________________________
Young working class males may find themselves committing crimes because they suffer from status frustration and are unable to achieve status through legal and legitimate means.

Answers: 1. Marxism, 2. functionalism, 3. Marxism, 4. feminism, 5. postmodernism, 6. Marxism, 7. feminism, 8. postmodernism, 9. functionalism

Applying research studies task

Features and behaviour of school subcultures

The following is an outline of some of the behaviours which are associated with school subcultures. Fill in the spaces with details of which sociologists and research studies could be used to illustrate these behaviours. Then fill in the last column by identifying whether the example you have given is pro or anti school/education. The first one is done for you.

Features/Behaviour	Sociologist/Research Study	Pro or Anti
Working hard	Shain – Faith Girls	Pro
Being rude to teachers		
Swearing and being loud/ aggressive		
Not doing the work		

Why school subcultures are formed

The following is an outline of some of the reasons why young people may form school subcultures. Fill in the spaces with details of which sociologists and studies could be used to illustrate these.

Reason	Sociologist/Research Study
Teacher racism	
Rebelling against parental culture	
Peer group culture	
To better themselves	
To gain status	

ExamCafé

Sociology of the family

Writing answers to part (a) questions

The part (a) question on the exam will always ask you to identify and explain two points. The question is worth 17 marks and these are all for skill AO1 – Knowledge and Understanding. This means that the examiners are looking for you to show a knowledge and understanding of key concepts, research studies, statistics and theories. You do not need to make criticisms in this part of the question or demonstrate evaluation skills. You should spend approximately 15 minutes on this part of the question.

Use the checklist below when practising these questions to ensure you gain maximum marks.

- Have I defined the key term(s)/concept(s) in the question? ☐
- Have I made two points? ☐
- Have I written a separate paragraph for each point? ☐
- Are the two points I have made clearly separated and different? ☐
- Have I referred to a piece of sociological research or a sociological theory in each paragraph? ☐
- Have I explained how this supports the point I am making? ☐
- Have I illustrated each point with an example and explained this? ☐

Good example

The following answer is a strong one as it covers all the points mentioned in the checklist above. Read the answer and highlight where the candidate has covered each point in the checklist.

(a) Identify and explain two ways in which family life may differ according to social class. (17 marks)

Student answer

Family life refers to the life or lifestyles of a group of people linked through blood or legal ties who normally live within the same household.

One way in which this may differ according to social class is in terms of the roles taken on by the men and women within the family. It has been argued by sociologists that domestic roles within middle class families tend to be more shared. Oakley's research showed that in middle class dual earner families, men and women tended to share more tasks and were in a better position to pay for extra help e.g. cleaners; whereas working class families tended to have more traditional divisions of labour with women taking on more responsibility for housework and childcare.

Another way in which family life may differ according to social class is that middle class families are seen as being more child-centred and concerned about their child's socialisation. King and Raynor argue that child-centredness is a feature of the middle class family and that middle class parents are particularly concerned with passing on the attitudes and opportunities required for educational success. Bourdieu argues that middle class children are given 'cultural capital' by their parents, which advantages them in education and life in general.

Example to improve

The example below could be improved. Using the checklist above try to identify what this answer does not do. Then rewrite the answer, covering all the points above.

(a) Identify and explain two ways in which an ageing population affects family life. (17 marks)

Student answer

One way in which an ageing population may affect family life is that it places an extra burden on family members, often the women. Grundy and Henretta argue that women see caring for elderly relatives as their duty. This responsibility often means they have less time to spend with their children and suffer the burden of paid work, housework, childcare, emotion work and care for elderly relatives.

Another way in which an ageing population may affect family life is that elderly relatives can provide free childcare for working parents. Elderly relatives can often be a positive resource for families rather than a burden.

Now try your own

Now try to write an answer to the question below. Remember to use the checklist as a guide. Ask your teacher to check your answer if you wish.

(a) Identify and explain two reasons for an increase in childless couples. (17 marks)

Writing answers to part (b) questions

The answer below is an example of a very strong answer. The numbers refer to a place where the candidate has demonstrated one of the sociological skills of either knowledge and understanding (AO1), interpretation and application (AO2a) or analysis and evaluation (AO2b). Read the answer and then fill in below which skill corresponds with which number.

(b) Outline and evaluate the view that the nuclear family benefits its members. (33 marks)

Student answer

The nuclear family is a family type made up of two parents and their children. It has also been referred to as the 'cereal packet family' as the image of a male breadwinner, female housewife and their two children was often shown in media advertising. Functionalist and new right sociologists argue that the nuclear family is the ideal family type and that it benefits its members. **1**

Functionalist sociologist Murdoch claims that the nuclear family benefits its members as it holds several important functions. Firstly, it holds an economic function in that the family both earns money and helps in the economy through buying consumer goods. Also, it holds an educational function because it socialises the children into the norms and values of society. And finally, it has sexual and reproductive functions. **2** This view is supported by Parsons who argues that the family has two main specialised functions: the socialisation of children and the stabilisation of adult personalities. His theory is also known as the 'warm bath theory' as he claims the family helps take away the stress of everyday life. This happens because the wife cares for the husband and looks after him when he returns from work and the husband plays with his children which helps him forget – it therefore has the relaxing effect of a warm bath. However, Murdoch and Parsons have been criticised for ignoring the dysfunctional aspects of family life. **3** Feminists argue that the family is not like a warm bath for the female in the household as she often has to go to work and care for all the members as well. Also, the functions the family provides can be provided by other institutions too.

Feminist sociologists would argue that the nuclear family does not benefit all its members and that men benefit from the family more than women. **4** Radical feminists claim that the family is a dangerous place for women as they often suffer from violence and rape at the hands of their husbands. The Council of Europe (2002) found that one in four women experience domestic violence in their lifetimes. **5** However, men can also be victims of domestic violence. **6** Statistics show that one in six men will be a victim of domestic violence at some point in their lives. Other feminists look at the unequal division of domestic tasks and childcare with women often taking responsibility for these even when they work full-time. Duncombe and Marsden argue that women often do a triple shift which involves paid work, housework, childcare and emotion work. However, this has changed and other research has shown that men are now doing a much greater share of housework and childcare.

Marxist sociologists suggest that the nuclear family does not benefit its members as much as it benefits capitalism. **7** The family helps maintain current and future generations of workers and keeps them fit and healthy so that they can work hard and therefore keep capitalism going. Zaretsky argues that family is a refuge from capitalism where workers can escape the boredom and stress of working within a capitalist society. Marxist feminists suggest that it is the women who suffer more from nuclear family life within capitalist societies as they are the slaves of wage slaves who perform domestic labour unpaid.

It is evident that the nuclear family may benefit its members in some ways or benefit particular members; for example, the male. However, there may be other family types which are more beneficial to their members. **8** Postmodernist sociologists point out that there is now a diverse range of family types that people can choose from including reconstituted, single parent and gay/lesbian. Dunne found that in lesbian families where the couple had children there was much greater sharing of housework and childcare tasks. It could be argued that such a set up is more beneficial for all members than the nuclear family.

Fill in your answers here:

1.	**5.**
2.	**6.**
3.	**7.**
4.	**8.**

Answers: 1. AO1, 2. AO1, 3. AO2b, 4. AO2a, 5. AO1, 6. AO2b, 7. AO2a, 8. AO2b

Writing introductions to part (b) questions

Good example

The following answer has the three clear components of an ideal introduction. It:

- defines key terms in the question
- identifies the view outlined in the question
- explains the view outlined in the question.

Read the example below and highlight where the student has covered the three points outlined above.

(b) Outline and evaluate the view that roles of men and women within the family have become more equal. (33 marks)

Student answer

Traditionally the roles between men and women within the family were separated by a gendered division of labour. Women would adopt the roles of caring wife and loving mother and men would take on the roles of breadwinner and protector. The view that argues that roles have become more equal comes from postmodernists such as Stacey (1996). She argues that the postmodern family is diverse and the individuals within the family choose which roles they want to adopt; this leads to the family roles being more equal.

Example to improve

The example below could be improved. Using the previous example as a guide, rewrite the introduction below making sure you cover the three components of a good introduction.

(b) Outline and evaluate the view that there now exists a range of family types in contemporary society. (33 marks)

Student answer

One of the family types that exist is the beanpole family; these families are long and thin. The beanpole family includes many generations and their ties are intergenerational rather than intra-generational.

Now try your own

Now have a go at writing an introduction to the question below. Make sure you cover the three components of a good introduction. Ask your teacher to check your answer if you wish.

(b) Outline and evaluate the view that the rising divorce rate since the 1970s is a direct consequence of changes in the law. (33 marks)

Writing conclusions to part (b) questions

Good Example

The following answer has the three clear components of a good conclusion. It:

- refers back to the actual wording in the question
- offers something new that has not already been mentioned in the answer e.g. a criticism or evaluative point
- makes a comment (i.e. actually concludes) on which argument there is the most evidence for/appears to be the strongest.

Read the example below and highlight where the candidate has covered the three points outlined above.

(b) Outline and evaluate the view that the rising divorce rate since the 1970s is a direct consequence of changes in the law. (33 marks)

Student answer

It is clear from the evidence discussed here that changes in the law may have had some impact on the rise in divorce rate since the 1970s. However, it cannot be the only factor. Changes in expectations, the decline in religious values and the impact of feminism have all played a part. More significantly, the divorce rate actually fell by 7% between 2005 and 2006, according to the ONS. Post modernist sociologists would argue that these more recent changes in the divorce rate may be of more interest to sociologists than the changes of the past.

Example to improve

The example below could be improved. Using the previous example as a guide, rewrite the conclusion below making sure you cover the three components of a good conclusion.

(b) Outline and evaluate the view that family life in contemporary Britain is in decline. (33 marks)

Student answer

In conclusion it is not possible to say whether the family is in decline or not. There is a lot of family diversity such as single parent families and reconstituted families; if this is the case then the different types of family show that it still exists.

Now try your own

Now have a go at writing a conclusion to the question below. Make sure you cover the three components of a good conclusion. Ask your teacher to check your answer if you wish.

(b) Outline and evaluate the view that the extended family no longer plays a significant role in family life in contemporary Britain. (33 marks)

ExamCafé

Sociology of health

Writing answers to part (a) questions

The part (a) question on the exam will always ask you to identify and explain two points. The question is worth 17 marks and these are all for skill AO1 – Knowledge and Understanding. This means that the examiners are looking for you to show a knowledge and understanding of key concepts, research studies, statistics and theories. You do not need to make criticisms in this part of the question or demonstrate evaluation skills. You should spend approximately 15 minutes on this part of the question.

Use the checklist below when practising these questions to ensure you gain maximum marks.

- Have I defined the key term(s)/concept(s) in the question? ☐
- Have I made two points? ☐
- Have I written a separate paragraph for each point? ☐
- Are the two points I have made clearly separated and different? ☐
- Have I referred to a piece of sociological research or a sociological theory in each paragraph? ☐
- Have I explained how this supports the point I am making? ☐
- Have I illustrated each point with an example and explained this? ☐

Good example

The following answer is a very strong one and covers all the points mentioned in the checklist above. Read the answer and highlight where the candidate has covered each point in the checklist.

(a) Identify and explain two features of the biomedical model of understanding health and illness. (17 marks)

Student answer

The biomedical model is a scientific approach to understanding health and illness. It is the view held by most health practitioners.

One feature of the biomedical model is that health is regarded as the absence of disease or disability. Hart argues that disease is seen as being something that is physically wrong with the body. The interaction of the social world and the individual are irrelevant. In this sense the biomedical model is a scientific approach which views ill health and disease separately from other factors.

Another feature of the biomedical model is that diagnoses of symptoms are seen as objective, requiring very little debate between the doctor and the patient. Sheeran argues that in the West medical professionals have been very successful in diagnosing and treating illnesses and injuries. For example, operations on broken bones, kidney transplants and caesarean sections are all very successful.

Example to improve

The example below could be improved. Using the checklist above try to identify what this answer does not do. Then rewrite the answer trying to cover all the points in the checklist.

(a) Identify and explain two trends in relation to health and gender. (17 marks)

Student answer

One trend in relation to health and gender is that women are more likely than men to experience neurotic disorders. They also receive far more prescriptions for tranquillisers, sleeping pills and antidepressants. Feminists argue that this is due to the stress and strain that women face in their roles as housewives and mothers as this role is not valued by society. They also suggest that women face more stress and demands in life as they are now expected to work full-time and take major responsibility for housework and childcare.

Brown et al found that the probability of depression increased when women felt trapped and humiliated.

Another trend in relation to health and gender is that women go to the doctor more often than men. Statistics show that women go to the doctor about fifty per cent more than men between the ages of 16 and 44.

Now try your own

Now try to write an answer to the question below. Remember to use the checklist as a guide. Ask your teacher to check your answer if you wish.

(a) Identify and explain two ways that becoming ill is a social process. (17 marks)

Writing answers to part (b) questions

The response below is an example of a very strong answer. The numbers refer to a place where the candidate has demonstrated one of the sociological skills of either knowledge and understanding (AO1), interpretation and application (AO2a) or analysis and evaluation (AO2b). Read the answer and then fill in below which skill corresponds with which number.

(b) Outline and evaluate the view that class inequalities in health are caused by structural factors. (33 marks)

Student answer

Statistical evidence shows that the lower your class background the more likely you are to suffer poor health. For example, according to the ONS men and women in social class V are twice as likely to die before reaching retirement age as people in social class I. **1** Structural explanations argue that these social class differences are caused by the structure of society and the different working/living conditions of the different classes.

Marxist sociologists argue that such health inequalities occur because in capitalist society the working class suffer from poverty and material deprivation which leads to poor health. Working class jobs are often more dangerous and involve longer working hours which bring more health risks. Also, working in repetitive jobs can cause workers to suffer from more stress related conditions. However, those working in positions of authority and responsibility are just as likely to suffer from stress at work. **2** Lobstein et al also argue that due to the low wages they receive the working class cannot afford a healthy diet.

However, social selection explanations offer a contradictory view to structural explanations. They claim that how good your health is will determine whether or not you move up or down the class ladder. Wadsworth showed that males who had a serious illness in their childhood were more likely to end up in a lower social class. The findings of Illsley support this. Illsley found that upwardly mobile females in Aberdeen were healthier, taller, had better physiques and lower death rates in their first pregnancies than those who were downwardly mobile. **3** However, this may simply be because their upwardly mobile status meant they had higher salaries and therefore could afford a healthier diet and lifestyle.

Cultural explanations on the other hand blame working class culture rather than the structure of society for the fact that the working class are more likely to suffer ill health. **4** They suggest it is the norms, values and lifestyle of the working class which leads to their ill health. HMSO reports suggest that people in the lower social classes indulge in more unhealthy behaviours such as smoking, drinking alcohol, eating more fat and sugar and taking less exercise. These behaviours lead to them being more likely to suffer from heart disease, cancer and asthma. However, cultural explanations have been criticised for blaming the victim. It may be that their disadvantaged position in society leads to these behaviours. **5** For example, a lack of money may cause stress which is relieved through drinking and smoking. Townsend argues that the more money you have the easier it is to adopt a healthy lifestyle; for example, to eat healthy foods and afford gym membership. **6**

It is clear that although structural explanations offer some insight into why class differences in health exist there are also other relevant explanations. **7** However, some sociologists question whether class differences in health actually exist at all. Comparisons which compare social class I with social class V are comparing two very small groups of people and could therefore exaggerate differences. Also, definitions of social class and also of different illnesses change over time and therefore comparisons may not be valid. **8**

Fill in your answers here:

1.	**5.**
2.	**6.**
3.	**7.**
4.	**8.**

Answers: 1. AO1, 2. AO2b, 3. AO1, 4. AO2a, 5. AO2b, 6. AO1, 7. AO2a, 8. AO1

Writing introductions to part (b) questions

Good Example

The following answer has the three clear components of an ideal introduction. It:

- defines key terms in the question
- identifies the view outlined in the question
- explains the view outlined in the question.

Read the example below and highlight where the student has covered the three points outlined above.

(b) Outline and evaluate the view that the working class are more likely to suffer ill health. (33 marks)

Student answer

The term working class is operationalised in an objective way by using the socio-economic classification model. Working class occupations are generally physically laborious; this can have a detrimental effect on the body, which can lead to the working classes experiencing greater ill health. Recent research carried out by the government in the form of the Wanless Report 2002 found that health inequalities exist between the social class groupings. The structural/materialist explanation argues that it is the structures of society that cause health inequalities; they argue that it is the way society is organised and not individual lifestyle choices that disadvantage the working class.

Example to improve

The example below could be improved. Using the previous example as a guide, rewrite the introduction below making sure you cover the three components of a good introduction.

(b) Outline and evaluate the view that the medical profession operates in the interest of the ruling class. (33 marks)

Student answer

Medical professionals blame ill health on the lifestyle choices of individuals. Medical professionals are seen as having a high status, therefore they control others. A sociologist said that doctors are rewarded with status and high financial rewards and therefore act as agents of social control for the ruling capitalist class.

Now try your own

Now have a go at writing an introduction to the question below. Make sure you cover the three components of a good introduction. Ask your teacher to check your answer if you wish.

(b) Outline and evaluate the view that health professionals have too much power in the contemporary UK. (33 marks)

Writing conclusions to part (b) questions

Good example

The following answer has the three clear components of a good conclusion. It:

- refers back to the actual wording in the question
- offers something new that has not already been mentioned in the answer, e.g. a criticism or evaluative point
- makes a comment (i.e. actually concludes) on which argument there is the most evidence for/appears to be the strongest.

Read the example below and highlight where the candidate has covered the three points outlined above.

(b) Outline and evaluate the view that ill health is a social construction. (33 marks)

Student answer

As discussed earlier, Interactionists would argue that health is a social construction and that we should be careful not to take the meaning of words such as 'health' and 'illness' for granted, as individuals attach different meanings to these words. Furthermore, as Interactionists argue, if health and illness were objective and scientific then there would be a homogeneous process of diagnoses and treatment. However, biological explanations have found that patterns of disease within certain ethnic groups can be the determining factor in an individual's ability to avoid ill health.

In conclusion the term ill health as Taylor et al (1996) identified is relative to a particular society. However, the postmodernist view does argue that the bio-medical model of health dominates societal views on what is ill health. Overall our individual perception of ill health is controlled to some extent by the biomedical model and the social construction of health is limited to the minority view of medical professionals.

Example to improve

The example below could be improved. Using the previous example as a guide, rewrite the conclusion below making sure you cover the three components of a good conclusion.

(b) Outline and evaluate the view that the biomedical model of health is no longer dominant in the contemporary UK. (33 marks)

Student answer

In conclusion the biomedical model is not as popular as it used to be as people are turning to alternative therapies to treat ill health.

Now try your own

Now have a go at writing a conclusion to the question below. Make sure you cover the three components of a good conclusion. Ask your teacher to check your answer if you wish.

(b) Outline and evaluate structural theories of gender inequality and health. (33 marks)

ExamCafé

Sociology of religion

Writing answers to part (a) questions

The part (a) question on the exam will always ask you to identify and explain two points. The question is worth 17 marks and these are all for skill AO1 – Knowledge and Understanding. This means that the examiners are looking for you to show a knowledge and understanding of key concepts, research studies, statistics and theories. You do not need to make criticisms in this part of the question or demonstrate evaluation skills. You should spend approximately 15 minutes on this part of the question.

Use the checklist below when practising these questions to ensure you gain maximum marks.

- Have I defined the key term(s)/concept(s) in the question? ☐
- Have I made two points? ☐
- Have I written a separate paragraph for each point? ☐
- Are the two points I have made clearly separated and different? ☐
- Have I referred to a piece of sociological research or a sociological theory in each paragraph? ☐
- Have I explained how this supports the point I am making? ☐
- Have I illustrated each point with an example and explained this? ☐

Good example

The following answer covers all the points mentioned in the checklist above. It was therefore awarded 17/17. Read the answer and highlight where the candidate has covered each point in the checklist.

(a) Identify and explain two reasons why religion is important to some ethnic groups. (17 marks)

Student answer

The term religion refers to beliefs, actions and institutions that assume the existence of supernatural entities with powers of action, or impersonal powers or processes possessed of moral purpose.

One reason that religion may be important to some ethnic groups is that it offers a sense of belonging and solidarity. Akhtar argues that this may be particularly relevant to young Muslims. He suggests that young Muslims may feel 'symbolically excluded' from British society and that religion gives them an alternative sense of belonging.

Another reason that religion may be important to some ethnic groups is that it helps unite them and fight racism. When some immigrant groups moved to Britain they were often faced with hostility from British people. Ballard and Ballard found that Sikhs who moved to Leeds from the Punjab often formed their own places of worship so that they could create their own communities of people with the same religious beliefs and ideas. These communities turned inwards and separated themselves from racist British society.

Example to improve

The example below was awarded 10 out of the possible 17 marks. Using the checklist above try to identify what this answer does not do. Then rewrite the answer, covering all points above, with the aim of getting 17/17.

(a) Identify and explain two types of New Religious Movements. (17 marks)

Student answer

One type of New Religious Movement (NRM) is a world rejecting movement. These movements cut themselves off from society and are often in conflict with society. Barker researched the Unification Church which is also known as the Moonies which is an example of a world rejecting NRM. She found that the Moonies required members to be totally committed and to change their lifestyles significantly. World rejecting movements often have a reputation for brainwashing their members.

Another type of NRM is world affirming movement. These movements are tolerant of other beliefs. An example of this is Scientology.

Now try your own

Now try to write an answer to the question below. Remember to use the checklist as a guide. Ask your teacher to check your answer if you wish.

(a) Identify and explain two functions of religion for society. (17 marks)

Writing answers to part (b) questions

The answer below is an example of a very strong answer. The numbers refer to a place where the candidate has demonstrated one of the sociological skills of either knowledge and understanding (AO1), interpretation and application (AO2a) or analysis and evaluation (AO2b). Read the answer and then fill in below which skill corresponds with which number.

(b) Outline and evaluate the view that religion can be a force for social change. (33 marks)

Student answer

Sociologists are interested in two kinds of social change; firstly, change to a whole society and secondly, change within a society. The view that religion can be a force for social change was argued by Max Weber and illustrated by his work on 'The Protestant Ethic and the Spirit of Capitalism'. **1**

In this book Weber tried to show how the religious ideas of Calvinists led to attitudes and behaviour that were favourable for the development of capitalism. The Calvinists saw work as a way of honouring God and believed that they should live life as simply as possible. This led to them being a thrifty, hard working group of people who gained enough capital to develop new ideas and inventions and therefore led to the development of capitalist modes of production. Weber therefore showed how religious ideas could lead to social change. However, Weber has been criticised by Parkin who claims that capitalism was late to develop in Scotland despite Calvinist Protestantism being present. **2**

Contemporary evidence also shows that religion can be a force for social change as some religious groups have used their religious beliefs and networks to actively campaign for social change. **3** Beckford uses the example of the Iranian revolution of 1979 where various political forces joined with Shia Muslims to expel the Shah and form an Islamic republic. Similarly, in the USA, Christian Black Power movements used their networks and power to campaign for change and improvements for black Americans.

However, not all sociologists agree that religion can be a force for social change. **4** Functionalist sociologist Durkheim believes that actually religion plays a key role in maintaining social order and value consensus. **5** He suggests that one of the key functions of religion is to socialise people into the existing norms and values of society and teach them a code of conduct for their behaviour. This ensures that the existing culture and order of society is maintained rather than social change occurring. However, functionalist sociologists have been criticised for ignoring the dysfunctional elements of religion; for example, the conflicts which occur between different religious groups in society. **6**

Marxist sociologists argue that rather than being a force for social change, religion is actually a tool used by capitalists to continue and to justify the exploitation of the working class. Religion acts as an agent of social control and they are kept in their place as they are led to believe that the position they hold is what God intended for them. **7** However, Hamilton criticises the idea that religion is manipulated by the ruling class as he suggests that often it springs from the working class themselves.

There is such a range of religious ideas in society today that it is difficult to come to a conclusion as to whether or not it is a force for social change. Some religious ideas can be both a force for social change but also conservative. For example, the Iranian revolution led to social change but brought in a regime which would prohibit any other change. **8** Also, other factors may need to be considered such as the existence of a charismatic leader or the availability of other channels through which people can solve their problems.

Fill in your answers here:

1.	**5.**
2.	**6.**
3.	**7.**
4.	**8.**

Answers: 1. AO1, 2. AO2b, 3. AO2a, 4. AO2b, 5. AO1, 6. AO2b, 7. AO1, 8. AO2a

Writing introductions to part (b) questions

Good Example

The following answer has the three clear components of an ideal introduction. It:

- defines key terms in the question
- identifies the view outlined in the question
- explains the view outlined in the question.

Read the example below and highlight where the student has covered the three points outlined above.

(b) Outline and evaluate the view that church attendance figures are an accurate indicator of religious belief. (33 marks)

Student answer

The term religious belief is normally associated with an individual who identifies themselves as being part of a religious faith where there is one God; this is evident in Christianity and the Islamic faith. Church attendance figures are measured by different organisations, such as the Christian charity 'Tearfund'. They believe that the statistics are a good indicator of religious belief, as measurement of participation and membership can be obtained.

Example to improve

The example below could be improved. Using the previous example as a guide, rewrite the introduction below making sure you cover the three components of a good introduction.

(b) Outline and evaluate the view that involvement with religion varies according to social characteristics. (33 marks)

Student answer

The middle classes are more likely to attend church due to the appeal of conservatism. Also the working class are less likely to go to church.

Now try your own

Now have a go at writing an introduction to the question below. Make sure you cover the three components of a good introduction. Ask your teacher to check your answer if you wish.

(b) Outline and evaluate the view that 'Religion is the opium of the people'. (33 marks)

Writing conclusions to part (b) questions

Good example

The following answer has the three clear components of a good conclusion. It:

- refers back to the actual wording in the question
- offers something new that has not already been mentioned in the answer e.g. a criticism or evaluative point
- makes a comment (i.e. actually concludes) on which argument there is the most evidence for/ appears to be the strongest.

Read the example below and highlight where the candidate has covered the three points outlined above.

(b) Outline and evaluate the view that there is much more religiosity in society than secularisation theorists acknowledge. (33 marks)

Student answer

Although Weber believed that religion would decline as society became more 'rational', surveys repeatedly show that while people may no longer go to church, they still profess a belief in God; this fits in with Davie's (1994) work on 'belief without belonging'. In conclusion religious practices and beliefs are changing. However, due to the lack of validity in measuring religiosity it is difficult to state clearly whether the secularisation theorists are correct.

Example to improve

The example below could be improved. Using the previous example as a guide, rewrite the conclusion below making sure you cover the three components of a good conclusion.

(b) Outline and evaluate the view that religion in general has negative consequences for women. (33 marks)

Student answer

In conclusion women see God in terms of love and comfort and men see God in terms of power and control. As men and women see God differently it cannot be said that religion is negative for women.

Now try your own

Now have a go at writing a conclusion to the question below. Make sure you cover the three components of a good conclusion. Ask your teacher to check your answer if you wish.

(b) Outline and evaluate the view that contemporary UK is a secular society. (33 marks)

ExamCafé

Sociology of youth

Writing answers to part (a) questions

The part (a) question on the exam will always ask you to identify and explain two points. The question is worth 17 marks and these are all for skill AO1 – Knowledge and Understanding. This means that the examiners are looking for you to show a knowledge and understanding of key concepts, research studies, statistics and theories. You do not need to make criticisms in this part of the question or demonstrate evaluation skills. You should spend approximately 15 minutes on this part of the question.

Use the checklist below when practising these questions to ensure you gain maximum marks.

- Have I defined the key term(s)/concept(s) in the question? ☐
- Have I made two points? ☐
- Have I written a separate paragraph for each point? ☐
- Are the two points I have made clearly separated and different? ☐
- Have I referred to a piece of sociological research or a sociological theory in each paragraph? ☐
- Have I explained how this supports the point I am making? ☐
- Have I illustrated each point with an example and explained this? ☐

Good example

The following answer covers all the points mentioned in the checklist above. It was therefore awarded 17/17. Read the answer and highlight where the candidate has covered each point in the checklist.

(a) Identify and explain two characteristics of youth subcultures. (17 marks)

Student answer

Youth subcultures are distinct groups within a wider mainstream culture who have their own norms and values, leisure interests, ways of dressing etc.

One characteristic of youth subcultures is that they often reject the norms and values of mainstream society. An example of this can be seen through the Rastafarian subculture which emerged in Britain in the 1970s. Rastafarians often wore the colours green, red and gold in tribute to Ethiopia. They engaged in deviant activities such as smoking weed. They listened to reggae music. Sivanadan argues that this subculture emerged in response to racism faced by young black males in the 1970s as it gave an identity to this group which was unique and did not involve white people.

Another characteristic of youth subcultures is that they tend to share a distinct way of dressing which differs from that of mainstream society. For example, the Punk subculture wore items such as bin liners, safety pins and tampons and turned them to clothing items. Hebdidge argues that Punks changed the meanings of these everyday items as a way of going against the norms of society. Other subcultures have a distinct way of dressing but this is purely for their own enjoyment. For example, Goths wear a lot of black and heavy make up. Hodkinson argues that there is no meaning behind this, it is simply a fun part of being a Goth.

Example to improve

The example below was awarded 10 out of the possible 17 marks. Using the checklist above try to identify what this answer does not do. Then rewrite the answer covering all points above with the aim of getting 17/17.

(a) Identify and explain two ways in which pupil subcultures may express anti-school values. (17 marks)

Student answer

One way in which pupil subcultures may express anti-school values is by being rude to teachers and other pupils. Paul Willis found these behaviours when studying 'the lads'. The lads were a group of working class boys who mucked around in class and bullied other boys who wanted to work hard. This was because they thought it was not masculine to study and also because they did not need qualifications to go on to do the same working class jobs that their fathers did.

Another way in which pupil subcultures may express anti-school values is by not going to school. Some working class girls do not go to school because they want to hang around and smoke and talk about boys instead.

Now try your own

Now try to write an answer to the question below. Remember to use the checklist as a guide. Ask your teacher to check your answer if you wish.

(a) Identify and explain two ways in which patterns of delinquent behaviour are linked to gender. (17 marks)

Writing answers to part (b) questions

The answer below is an example of a very strong answer. The numbers refer to a place where the candidate has demonstrated one of the sociological skills of either knowledge and understanding (AO1), interpretation and application (AO2a) or analysis and evaluation (AO2b). Read the answer and then fill in below which skill corresponds with which number.

(b) Outline and evaluate the view that delinquency arises from the values of working class culture. (33 marks)

Student answer

Delinquency is a criminal or antisocial act committed by juveniles (those aged between 10 and 17). Research shows that the lowest social classes have the highest crime rates. Wallamsley et al found that 41% of prisoners are from the lowest social classes even though only 19% of the population belong to such classes. **1** The Youth Lifestyles Survey (1999) found that the lowest social classes were more likely to be persistent or serious offenders. The functionalist sociologist, Walter Miller, argues that this is because delinquency arises from the values of working class culture. **2**

Miller claims that deviant behaviour is not a response to the situation of the working class but instead is caused by the values of their culture. For example, the working class concern for masculinity leads them to reject timid and weak behaviour and may lead them to be involved in fighting. He refers to this as the value of 'toughness'. He suggests that the working class are also hedonistic and search for 'thrills' through gambling, sexual adventure and drinking. He refers to this as the value of excitement. He states that the working class are fatalistic and accept that nothing can be done about their lives and this means they do not worry about getting involved in crime. However, Miller's theory has been criticised as the values that he outlines could also apply to the middle classes. **3** There is evidence of super rich city workers also seeking excitement, drinking heavily and taking drugs. Also, not all working class people are delinquent, it is only a small proportion of the population.

Functionalist sociologist Albert Cohen puts forward an alternative argument. Rather than suggesting that delinquency arises from the values of working class culture, he suggests it is a response to 'status deprivation'. **4** He says that working class males feel looked down upon by society and are denied status through jobs and education. They therefore develop an alternative set of values within their peer group which gives them status. These values are often related to delinquent behaviour. However, Cohen has been criticised by feminist sociologists for failing to explain female delinquency and only looking at the experience of males. They refer to theories such as this as 'male stream sociology'. **5**

On the other hand, another reason why the working class may be more delinquent and likely to commit crime could be due to deprivation. Coles argues that there is a clear link between material and social deprivation and levels of offending. This is supported by Marxist sociologists Lea and Young who argue that relative deprivation, i.e. not having enough money, leads people to commit crime.

In conclusion, there are clearly several possible explanations for working class delinquency other than that it arises from working class culture. **6** However, it must also be considered that the working class may not actually commit more crime as official statistics may reflect patterns of policing and therefore be biased. **7** It is possible that deprived areas are more heavily patrolled than middle class ones and therefore delinquent behaviour is more likely to be identified. Graham and Bowling interviewed a range of young people and found that middle class children were just as likely to commit crime as working class children. **8**

Fill in your answers here:

1.	5.
2.	6.
3.	7.
4.	8.

Answers: 1. AO1, 2. AO2a, 3. AO2b, 4. AO2a, 5. AO2b, 6. AO2a, 7. AO2b, 8. AO1

Writing introductions to part (b) questions

Good example

The following answer has the three clear components of an ideal introduction. It:

- defines key terms in the question
- identifies the view outlined in the question
- explains the view outlined in the question.

Read the example below and highlight where the student has covered the three points outlined above.

(b) Outline and evaluate the view that distinctive youth subcultures are less significant for young people in the contemporary UK. (33 marks)

Student answer

The term 'youth subcultures' is used by sociologists to refer to groups who share different norms, values, style and interests from those of the mainstream culture. The view that these subcultures are less significant for young people in the contemporary UK is that of postmodernist sociologists. Postmodernists claim that there is too much diversity in the contemporary UK for one distinctive youth subculture to be identified.

Example to improve

The example below could be improved. Using the previous example as a guide, rewrite the introduction below making sure you cover the three components of a good introduction.

(b) Outline and evaluate the view that ethnic minorities are over-represented as delinquent. (33 marks)

Student answer

Those from ethnic minority groups are over-represented as delinquent. It is likely that ethnic minority groups are penalised and stereotyped. The police target ethnic minorities and have stereotyped views of them.

Now try your own

Now have a go at writing an introduction to the question below. Make sure you cover the three components of a good introduction. Ask your teacher to check your answer if you wish.

(b) Outline and evaluate the view that pupils' subcultures are a response to the school experiences of some groups of pupils. (33 marks)

Writing conclusions to part (b) questions

Good Example

The following answer has the three clear components of a good conclusion. It:

- refers back to the actual wording in the question
- offers something new that has not already been mentioned in the answer e.g. a criticism or evaluative point
- makes a comment (i.e. actually concludes) on which argument there is the most evidence for/appears to be the strongest.

Read the example below and highlight where the candidate has covered the three points outlined above.

(b) Outline and evaluate the view that the function of youth culture is to assist in the transition from childhood to adulthood. (33 marks)

Student answer

Although there is evidence from functionalist sociologists to support the idea that the function of youth culture is to assist in the transition from childhood to adulthood it cannot be that this is the only function or a function for everyone. Feminist sociologists would argue that we do not know if youth culture has this function for girls as they have been neglected from the male stream research. It can therefore be concluded that this may be one of its functions but more research would have to be carried out before it could be argued that this is the case.

Example to improve

The example below could be improved. Using the previous example as a guide, rewrite the conclusion below making sure you cover the three components of a good conclusion.

(b) Outline and evaluate the view that boys' ideas of masculinity affect their experience of schooling. (33 marks)

Student answer

In conclusion, there is no pattern of masculinity which is found everywhere; the journey which boys take to become a man is unpredictable. All boys act with masculinity in different ways.

Now try your own

Now have a go at writing a conclusion to the question below. Make sure you cover the three components of a good conclusion. Ask your teacher to check your answer if you wish.

(b) Outline and evaluate the view that working class youths commit crime because they are disadvantaged. (33 marks)

Conclusion

Top ten tips for the exam

1. Ensure that your class notes are in order; it might be helpful to use dividers to separate your notes on each Unit.

2. It is a good idea to keep testing yourself to see what you can remember and then to make a note of those points that you are struggling with. You can then go over them and test yourself again.

3. Try out a range of revision techniques to see which is most effective for you (see the introduction to this book for ideas on how to revise effectively).

4. Make sure you are familiar with the exam paper layout and that you carefully read not only the assessment questions but the instructions as well; this will ensure that your response includes everything that it should.

5. Take note of the total marks for each part of the question; this will help you decide on how long you should spend on each part of the overall question.

6. Do plenty of practice exam questions; this is not only useful in terms of checking your knowledge, but it will also allow you to check your timing. You must ensure that you can write a full response in the time allocated.

7. If you are concerned that you may forget information when you get into the exam, then it is a good idea to write any information down, e.g. sociologists' names, concepts etc., as soon as you are given permission to write in the exam.

8. Make sure that you plan your answer before you write it, particularly for those questions which are worth the greatest amount of marks.

9. Once you have completed your answers, it is worth taking the time to read over them again, to see if you can develop them further and to check for any errors or points that you may have missed.

10. Once you have finished the exam and have left the exam venue try not to think about the answers you have given. Be confident that if you have put in the hard work during your AS year and you have revised effectively by following the tips and activities in this book then you should be successful.

Unit 2 Answers: Topics in socialisation, culture and identity

Please note the page references below refer to where you can find the study in the accompanying textbook – *OCR Sociology AS* by Waugh et al

Sociology of the family: Applying research studies task

Beanpole families	Brannen (2003) *page 135*
Co-parenting	Smart (2000) *page 136*
Same sex families	Weeks et al (1999) *page 138*
Emotion work	Duncombe and Marsden (1995) *page 146*
Domestic violence	Dobash and Dobash (2000) *page 148*
Dads	Hatter et al (2002) *page 149*
Ageing population	Grundy and Henretta (2006) or Allan and Crow (2001) *page 152*

Sociology of health: Applying research studies task

Disease	Taylor et al (1996) *page 157*
Health	Dubos (1987) or Illich (2002) *page 156*
Biomedical model of health	Taylor and Field (2007) *page 158*
Mental illness	MIND *page 186*
Disability	DDA *page 194*
Alternative medicine	Hunt and Lightly (1999) *page 204*
Orthodox medicine	Hunt and Lightly (1999) *page 205*

Sociology of religion: Applying research studies task

Symbolic exclusion	Akhtar (2005) *page 230*
New Age movements	Drane (1999) *page 216* or Bruce (2005) *page 234*
Secularisation	Bruce (2002) *page 236* or Wilson (1976) *page 239*
Religious pluralism	Wilson (1976) *page 239*
Spirituality	Heelas (1996) *page 216*
Religion – inclusive definition	Durkheim (1912) or Geetz (1966) *page 209*
Religion – exclusive definition	Bruce (2002) *page 209*

Sociology of Youth: Applying research studies task

All studies can be found on Pages 276–278 of *OCR Sociology AS* by Waugh et al

Features and behaviour of school subcultures

Features/Behaviour	Sociologist/Research Study	Pro or Anti
Working hard	Shain (2003) – Faith Girls	Pro
	Sewell (2000) – Conformists	Pro
	Shain (2003) – The Survivors	Pro
Being rude to teachers	Shain (2003) Gang Girls	Anti
	Archer & Yamashati (2003) Harkton Boys	Anti
	Sewell (2000) Retreatists and Rebels	Anti
Swearing and being loud/aggressive	Archer and Yamashati (2003) Harkton Boys	Anti
	Jackson (2006) Ladettes	Anti
Not doing the work	Jackson (2006) Ladettes	Anti
	Sewell (2000) Retreatists and Rebels	Anti

Why school subcultures are formed

Reason	Sociologist/Research Study
Teacher Racism	Sewell (2000) Innovators
	Shain (2003) Survivors and Gang Girls
Rebelling against parental culture	Shain (2003) Rebels
Peer group culture	Archer and Yamashati (2003)
	Sewell (2000) Rebels
	Shain (2003) Gang Girls
To better themselves	Sewell (2000) Conformists
	Shain (2003) The Survivors
To gain status	Archer and Yamashati (2003) Harkton Boys
	Sewell (2000) Rebels